30 Days to a Clean

and Organized House

By Katie Berry

First digital edition 2014

First trade paperback edition, second digital edition 2015

ISBN-13: 978-1508564966

ISBN-10: 1508564965

CONTENTS

INTRODUCTION

If you've been battling home clutter and messes for any length of time, this is probably not the first book you've turned to for help. Maybe you have a shelf of books that have promised a total home transformation but which only offered vague advice. Maybe you have books that seemed to make sense but required you to buy a number of containers, baskets, and other products before you could get started.

This is not one of those books.

On my website, HousewifeHowTos.com, I've spent years helping others learn to efficiently cook, clean, get organized, do laundry, and save money. Often when people leave a comment or send me an email they're at their wit's end.

Here are just a few things readers have shared with me:

> *I can spend all day cleaning but it looks like I haven't done a thing.*

> *There are piles of junk everywhere and I feel like I'm just shoveling them from one place to another.*

> *Last Spring I cleaned my whole house. I so proud! Two weeks later it was back to the same mess.*

> *I spend so much time cleaning house but my bedroom looks like a dump. There's never enough time to take care of MY space.*

> *I work long hours and hate spending my whole weekend cleaning. My house shows it, too. I can't keep living like this but don't know how to fix it, either.*

If this sounds familiar, you're not alone. We all wish cleaning and organizing could be as simple as the advice the King gives to the White Rabbit in Alice in Wonderland: "Begin and the beginning and go on till you come to the end: then stop."

Scores of books about cleaning and organizing make it sound that simple: start with one thing, keep going, and then you're done. Actually that linear approach is what causes the problem!

Books which tell you that cleaning is a matter of going from Point A to Point B to Point C ignore that, when it comes to cleaning and organization, there's no such thing as being completely done. There is, however, a way to do things methodically so you not only clean and organize a room but keep it clean and organized, too.

How This Book Is Different

This book will keep you from getting lost. With *30 Days to a Clean and Organized House* you will learn to clean and organize, yes, but you will also learn to keep your home in great shape by taking a little time every day to maintain what you've done.

As you work through the book you'll see that each day has three parts to it: cleaning, organizing and maintaining. It's important to understand these are three distinct steps.

Cleaning consists of wiping, dusting, scrubbing, vacuuming, etc. It also involves tossing what's obviously trash (food wrappers, old newspapers, dead floral arrangements) but not sorting through or arranging things.

Organizing means to sort through items, decide where they belong, and then put them there.

Maintaining, the final step, involves returning to rooms you've already cleaned and organized to restore them to their pristine condition.

Once you've finished the plan you'll have cleaned and organized every room, cupboard, and closet. You will also have *kept* them clean and organized throughout the entire 30 days. Then, using the Monthly Routine, you'll be able to keep your home *just as clean and organized* in less time than you're probably spending now.

The #1 Rule

There is an inner logic to this plan. The days are arranged in a specific order to provide maximum impact for your cleaning efforts. Each day's tasks are laid out to build on what you've already accomplished, and what you'll be doing next. Even the steps in each task are structured to help you work efficiently. Change any of these things and you'll wind up going down the rabbit hole.

So the #1 Rule is *trust the plan.*

Following the plan as-written addresses the main rooms in your home first, even if the others are messier. Why? Because when the rooms where you spend the majority of your time begin to feel serene and organized it will give you the motivation to keep going until your entire house is clean.

Meanwhile, your family will begin to appreciate the changes to your home and they'll help maintain them. You might even find they're willing to help with each day's tasks, and since the plan is so straightforward they'll be able to!

Don't believe me? Here are some things readers of the Kindle version of this book have already said in their reviews:

> ➤ *This 30 day plan is different. It's simple, straightforward, well organized and not the least bit gushy or preachy. It's practical enough that even my husband is on board.*

> ➤ *I've dabbled with a lot of cleaning and home organizational methods, hoping that one would finally take hold and help me conquer the beast. I'm impressed with this one. Gave my daughter the list for cleaning the living room, and it looked the best it had in a long time.*

> ➤ *With my overloaded schedule, I never thought I could achieve such a clean and organized home (including Kids rooms)! AMAZINGLY......it stays clean and organized with the help of your Daily Tidy Up routine!*

Rearranging or skipping any of the steps in this plan is what takes people down that rabbit hole where they spend hours working but have nothing to show for it. So *do not* skip a step and *do not* rearrange the days just because you'd rather clean your office before your laundry room. Trust the plan.

Work At Your Own Pace

While it's important that you work through the days in order -- and work each day as outlined -- there is no reason you have to do the plan in thirty days. Maybe you have physical limitations which require you to rest between bouts of activity. Maybe you work insane hours and only have a half-hour per day to deal with your house. Maybe you just like to take things nice and slow. Work the plan at your own pace, but whatever you do, *work in the order provided.*

Remember, this is not a competition. You absolutely do not want to get burned out. Spending some time working on the plan's steps each and every day will accomplish wonders in your home. How quickly that happens really is up to you.

The Daily Cleaning Routine

The Daily Cleaning Routine is the foundation for everything you're going to accomplish in the next thirty days. Following the Daily Cleaning Routine will take you through the majority of your home where you'll tackle messes and clutter before they become a problem. For some people, this step alone makes a *huge* transformation in their home's cleanliness and comfort, one which restores their confidence and motivation.

Don't let the name of the routine frighten you! By "daily cleaning" I do *not* mean scrubbing your floors and polishing your windows every

9

single day. Who has the time or energy for that? A daily cleaning routine just means spending a half-hour or less establishing a baseline.

Important note: If you haven't cleaned in a while, it's going to take you longer than a half-hour to go through the daily routine the first time. It might even take a few hours. After that I promise you'll get it down to a half-hour or less, and you will absolutely love how your home looks!

The Daily Cleaning Routine Checklist

BEDROOM:

- Make your bed every morning. A rumpled bed will make even the cleanest rooms look like a disaster.
- Pick up all clothing. Clean stuff gets folded or hung; dirty stuff goes in the hamper.
- Put away jewelry, hand lotion, and other items on the nightstand.
- Check the floor. Vacuum or dry mop high-traffic areas as needed.

BATHROOM:

- Wipe the sink basin clean.
- Buff water spots from mirror and faucet.
- Wipe the toilet seat and rim with a disinfecting cloth.
- Spray the shower, tub and shower door/curtain with homemade daily shower spray. (See the chapter on "Homemade Cleaning Mixes" for the recipe.)
- Replace any makeup-stained towels or wash cloths with clean ones.
- Check the floor. Sweep as needed.

KITCHEN:

- Empty the dishwasher if it's full.
- Empty the sink of any dirty dishes, and give the sink a quick scrub.
- Spray and wipe down counters and appliance fronts.
- Corral any clutter into a neat pile to deal with later in the day.
- Use a damp cloth to clean any splatters on the floor.
- Set out a clean dishtowel.
- Microwave your wet sponge for 60 seconds, or run it through the dishwasher, to disinfect it.
- Give the floor a quick sweep.

LIVING AND/OR FAMILY ROOM:

- Straighten all pillows and blankets on the sofa, which is one of the room's major focal points.
- Tidy magazines, books, games and DVDs.
- Wipe away any obvious crumbs and fingerprints from table tops.
- Take dishes to kitchen and put them in the dishwasher.
- Check the floor. Use a carpet sweeper or hand vacuum to pick up any messes.

Daily Cleaning Routine

Bedrooms

Make bed
Put dirty clothes in hamper
Hang or fold clean clothes
Straighten nightstand
Check floor

Bathrooms

Wipe sink basins
Buff spots on mirrors
Shine faucets
Wipe toilet handle then seat
with disinfecting cloth
Spray shower and tub with
daily shower spray
Check floor
Change towels if dirty

Living Room

Straighten cushions, pillows
Fold throw blankets
Tidy magazines, DVDs,
and games
Wipe coffee and end tables
Check floor
Take dishes to kitchen

Kitchen

Empty dishwasher
Empty and scrub sink
Shine faucet
Remove counter clutter
Wipe counters and appliance
fronts
Wipe spots on floor
Microwave wet sponge
Set out clean towel

THE 30-DAY PLAN

"Nothing will work unless you do."

– Coach John Wooden

DAY ONE

Today's cleaning task: The Daily Cleaning Routine

Don't get discouraged by how long this routine takes today — I promise it *will* get faster! Think about it: if your bathroom vanities and mirrors are coated in grime today, and the coffee table is covered in food smears, it's going to take a good amount of time to fix those things. But it's almost impossible for them to be as messy tomorrow, so will take less time, and every day you do the routine it will get faster.

Today's organizing task: Spice Cupboard or Drawer

Did you know that herbs and spices have a shelf life? Check to see if yours are still fresh, or whether it's time to replace them. You can tell with a good sniff: the stronger the aroma, the fresher they are. Faint fragrance means faint flavor, so replace those that don't have much oomph.

In the future, consider writing the date of purchase on the bottom of new bottles. Here's how long they'll last:

- Ground spices (cinnamon, cloves, etc.): 2 to 3 years
- Whole spices (whole nutmeg, cinnamon sticks, peppercorns): 4 years
- Dried Herbs (sage, thyme, parsley): 1 to 3 years
- Seeds (poppy, sesame, mustard): 2 years
- Seasoning mixes (taco, seasoning salt): 1 to 2 years
- Extracts (vanilla, peppermint, almond) 4 years

Today's maintenance task: The Laundry

Do everything in your power to get ALL of the laundry done today and you'll be lightening your load for the rest of the month.

If the thought of sorting and washing mounds of laundry is too overwhelming then plan on catching up by doing at least one load per day *in addition to* laundry scheduled as part of each day's tasks.

DAY TWO

Today's Cleaning Task: Refrigerator

A clean refrigerator makes cooking more pleasant and is critical for food safety. This appliance houses your family's favorite beverages and snacks, which raw foods can contaminate. So grab a trash can, some microfiber cloths, and your cleaning products, and get to it. (See the chapter on "Homemade Cleaning Mixes" to make your own.)

1.   **Remove everything from the refrigerator:** Toss expired items into the trash or compost, and put items you'll be keeping into coolers. (Maintaining proper food temperature while you're cleaning is essential to food safety!)

14

2.   **Remove refrigerator shelves and drawers:** Wash them in a sink of hot, soapy water. Use baking soda to scrub tough spills. Dry them.

3.   **Wash the interior:** Fill a bowl with warm, soapy water and stir in some baking soda. Dip a microfiber cloth into the liquid, wring well, and wipe down the interior of the fridge to deodorize and clean it simultaneously. Be sure to rinse your cloth frequently!

4.   **Clean the fridge gasket:** This is easily done using a soft toothbrush dipped into the soapy water. You may need to carefully pry the gasket open with your fingertips to remove stubborn spills.

5.   **Put it back together:** Return the clean, dry shelves and drawers to the refrigerator. Close the fridge.

6.   **Pull the empty fridge from the wall:** If you have back problems, please get help doing this. Unplug the fridge.

7.   **Clean the hidden parts:** Dust the wall behind the fridge then sweep and mop the floor beneath it. Vacuum the grill and/or coils. Empty and wash the drain pan in hot soapy water, then dry and reinstall it.

8.   **Plug the fridge in and push it back into place:** Clean the exterior, including the top, with hot soapy water.

9.   **Let it chill:** Allow the empty fridge to chill for 1 hour before transferring food back from the coolers. If you cut corners and just put your food on the kitchen counter, get it back into the fridge immediately and do NOT open the refrigerator for any reason for the next hour!

Today's Organizing Task: Beneath the Kitchen Sink

- Pull everything from beneath the kitchen sink and give the cupboard a good scrub. If your pipes are exposed, wipe them down as well.

- Sort through the cupboard contents before returning them to place, discarding things you no longer use and returning items that belong elsewhere. Note on your grocery list any items that need refills.
- Return items to the cupboard.

Today's Maintenance Task: Daily Cleaning Routine (Emphasis on Bedrooms)

While doing the Daily Cleaning Routine, spend some extra time in the bedroom. Although not as thorough as a weekly cleaning, which we'll get to later, these steps will help set a baseline of cleanliness for your bedrooms.

- Dust the tops of dressers and nightstands.
- Change the sheets.
- Give the room a good wall-to-wall vacuuming.

DAY THREE

Today, and every day for the rest of this 30-Day Plan, you'll be getting rid of clutter. Note the operative phrase there: you are *getting rid* of these things, not merely shuffling them from one room to another.

As you follow the plan, you'll be discarding trash in each room of your house as well as donating unwanted items. It's essential that, no matter how tired you are, you take the trash out and put the box of items for donation into your car.

Once a week, you'll be making a trip to drop off your donation boxes at your favorite local charity. This follow-through step is the payoff for the effort you've put in -- without it you've just moved junk around but haven't really purged any clutter or trash.

Today's Cleaning Task: Freezer

1.   **Remove everything from the freezer**: Toss expired items into the trash or compost. Place items you'll be keeping into coolers. (Maintaining proper food temperature while you're cleaning is essential to food safety!)

2.   **If you have an automatic ice maker, dump the cubes:** Ice acquires a stale taste after a while, and you may find your ice drawer actually collects crumbs. Wash the drawer in warm, soapy water and allow it to dry.

> *Bonus Tip: If you have a garbage disposal, run the ice cubes through it to remove gunk from the disposal blades.*

3.   **Remove freezer shelves and drawers:** Wash them in soapy water. Use baking soda to scrub tough spills. Dry them.

4.   **Clean the interior:** Fill a bowl with hot, soapy water and stir in some baking soda. Dip a microfiber cloth into the liquid, wring well, and wipe down the interior of the freezer to clean and deodorize it simultaneously. Be sure to rinse your cloth frequently!

5.   **Clean the freezer gasket:** Again, use a soft toothbrush dipped into the soapy water with baking soda. You may need to carefully pry the gasket open with your fingers to remove stubborn spills.

6.   **Put it back together:** Return the clean, dry shelves and drawers to the freezer. Close it.

7.   **Let it chill:** Allow the freezer an hour to reach the appropriate temperature before you transfer food back into it. If you cut corners and just put your food on the kitchen counter, get it back into the freezer immediately, and do NOT open the freezer door for any reason for the next hour!

Today's Organizing Task: The Junk Drawer

Every house has a junk drawer that started as a handy place to keep pens, tape, or a screwdriver handy. Then one thing led to another and, boom, the drawer was bulging with junk. Today we're going to make that drawer less frustrating and more functional. A tidy "junk drawer" is actually a small but important victory against clutter!

1.   **Empty it:** Spread a newspaper or towel over your kitchen counter and dump the contents of the drawer on it.

2.   **Wipe it:** Clean the inside of the drawer with a damp microfiber cloth.

3.   **Remove clutter:** Test any pens you find in your junk pile. Toss the ones that don't work, and gather the rest with a rubber band.

4.   **Organize it:** Gather things like batteries or paperclips and stash them in separate clear sandwich bags before returning them to the drawer. Use sandwich twist ties to keep phone chargers and headphone cords from getting tangled in the drawer.

5.   **Toss trash:** Look at what's left on the counter and throw away any trash.

6.   **Put things away:** The remaining things on the counter most likely belong in a different room. Group them based on the room where they belong and return each group to its proper location. Don't let them just sit around or you'll be making more work for yourself tomorrow!

7.   **Shut it:** Put your clean and newly organized Junk Drawer back in place.

Today's Maintenance Task: Daily Cleaning (Emphasis on Bathrooms)

Give the bathrooms a bit of extra attention today as you do the Daily Cleaning Routine. The steps below, combined with those listed in the daily routine, amount to a weekly bathroom cleaning:

- Disinfect and scrub the toilet bowl.
- Wipe the exterior of the toilet.
- Clean the tub and shower.
- Sweep or vacuum and then mop the floor.
- Empty the trash.
- Wash the dirty towels.

  Bonus Tip: Washing a room's linens the same day you clean the room will help keep laundry from taking over your house.

DAY FOUR

By now you're seeing the power of the Daily Cleaning Routine. While cleaning and organizing the refrigerator, freezer, junk drawer and spice drawer are largely unnoticed tasks, the Daily Cleaning Routine is already transforming your home. Now it's time for one final hidden cleaning task in the kitchen: the pantry.

A well-organized pantry can be a wonderful money-saver since it lets you stock up on your family's favorite foods when they're on sale. It can also save time. By grouping multiples of items together in a container, and organizing things by function, you'll be able to grab what you need without having to rummage through your shelves.

On the other hand, an unorganized pantry wastes money since you'll buy duplicates of items you already have. If it's disorganized enough, you may wind up throwing away food that's expired or gone stale.

Since this is a fairly complicated cleaning task, there's a flowchart following the checklist. I *strongly encourage* you to read through the checklist for explanation of each step, even if you plan to use the flowchart.

Today's Cleaning Task: Pantry

1.   **Clear the shelves from top to bottom:**

- *Throw away:* Move the trashcan close to your pantry shelves and begin emptying the pantry, starting at the top. Toss expired and stale foods, including cereal or cracker boxes that weren't closed properly. Make a note of items you need to replace.
- *Donate:* If you have canned goods you know your family will never eat (like the lima beans that sat on my shelves for 6 months), put them in a bag to give to your local food pantry.

2.   **Clean the bare shelves:** Carefully scrape up any sticky spills with a spoon. Sprinkle on baking soda to absorb the mess then wipe clean using warm, soapy water. Let dry then sweep or vacuum away any crumbs. Be sure to look in the corners and under shelves for cobwebs.

3.   **Line the shelves if you want:** Adhesive shelf linings tend to lift at the corners where they attract crumbs and, eventually, bugs. If you're partial to shelf-liner, use wax or parchment paper instead. Cut it to fit, wrapping it over the front of the shelf if you like, and use push-pins to hold it in place. Now you can easily clean messes and replace the liner when needed.

4.   **Corral the clutter:** Gather similar items in containers (e.g., oatmeal packets or envelopes of dressing mix). Don't let perfectionism get in the way here: while decorative organizing containers are nice to have, the important thing is actually getting organized. Use plastic sandwich bags, Mason jars, food storage containers, etc. You can always replace them with fancy canisters later -- for now, just get organized!

20

5.   **Group items to save time:** First, group items by function: baking items (flour, baking soda, etc.) belong on the same shelf together so you can find recipe ingredients easily. Next, group multiples together (e.g., cans of diced tomatoes, boxes of pasta, etc.) so you know how many of an item you have left. Put the oldest items toward the front so you use them up first.

6.   **Clean items as you return them to the shelves:** Wipe down bottles and boxes so you aren't returning messy, dusty things to your clean pantry. As you work, keep in mind how you actually use the things in your pantry: items you don't use very often should go the highest shelves, while things you use frequently should be easy to grab. To keep your kids from tearing apart the pantry put their snacks where they can see them.

Pantry Cleaning Routine

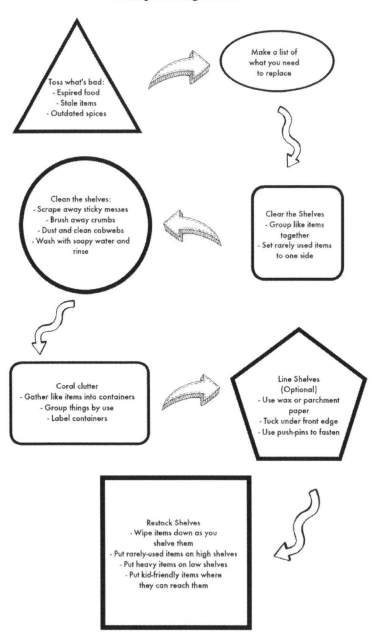

Toss what's bad:
- Espired food
- Stale items
- Outdated spices

Make a list of what you need to replace

Clear the Shelves
- Group like items together
- Set rarely used items to one side

Clean the shelves:
- Scrape away sticky messes
- Brush away crumbs
- Dust and clean cobwebs
- Wash with soapy water and rinse

Coral clutter
- Gather like items into containers
- Group things by use
- Label containers

Line Shelves (Optional)
- Use wax or parchment paper
- Tuck under front edge
- Use push-pins to fasten

Restock Shelves
- Wipe items down as you shelve them
- Put rarely-used items on high shelves
- Put heavy items on low shelves
- Put kid-friendly items where they can reach them

Today's Organizing Task: Food Storage Container Cupboard

Every kitchen seems to have a cupboard where food storage containers and lids get shoved, one which often causes an avalanche every time someone opens the door. If you're short on help cleaning up after meals, the hassle of dealing with the food storage container cupboard might be why!

1.   **Empty it:** Put everything on the counter.

2.   **Wipe it:** Clean the interior of the empty cupboard with a microfiber cloth dipped in warm, soapy water. Use a baking soda paste to scrub stubborn stains or spills. Follow with another cloth dipped in clean water and allow the cupboard to air dry.

3.   **Sort the contents:** Match up same-sized containers and make sure you have lids for each. Set aside any stained containers; you'll clean them after the cupboard is organized.

4.   **Toss the trash:** Throw away (or recycle) any lids that don't fit your containers, and any containers without lids. Also discard containers where the plastic or the lid has bubbled; they're no longer food safe and can actually add harmful substances to your food.

Bonus tip: Use lidless containers to hold small items in your pantry, and use lids without containers under potted plants to catch drips.

5.   **Clean the contents:** Scrub stains from plastic containers with a paste of baking soda, salt and water. If the stain remains, squeeze some lemon juice on it and set the container in the sun. (Use some common sense and don't put plastic on cement or metal surfaces outside when the temps are over 90° F.)

6.   **Organize it:** Group your same-sized containers, with their lids, and return them to the cupboard.

7.   **Now, keep it straight!** Next time you're emptying the dishwasher, take the extra time to put containers and their lids away properly. When you're trying to find a container for your leftovers after dinner you'll be glad you took that extra time!

Today's Maintenance Task: Daily Cleaning (Emphasis on Laundry Room)

When you've finished the Daily Cleaning Routine, spend a few extra minutes giving the laundry room some attention. This is not a deep-cleaning -- we'll get to that. The purpose of today's maintenance task is simply to get you in the habit of including your laundry room in your weekly chores.

If you've been good about following this plan, you got caught up on laundry just a few days ago, and laundered towels yesterday so your laundry room should be nice and empty. If you ignored these steps, you're about to see why it's important to follow the plan in order!

- Wipe the top of the washer and dryer.
- Scrub the dryer's lint screen with hot, soapy water. Air dry.
- Grab a microfiber cloth and quickly dust the shelves.
- Give the floor a quick sweep and you're done.

DAY FIVE

This week's focus on the kitchen has transformed the behind-the-scenes spaces in your kitchen. Now it's time to clean the rest of your appliances.

Today's Cleaning Task: Stove, Oven and Microwave

1.   **Start with the stove:** Wash it using hot, soapy water and a microfiber cloth. Clean dirty stove-eyes and glass or ceramic cook tops using a toothbrush dipped into a paste of baking soda and water. Rinse well with hot water to remove any residue.

2.   **Tend to details:** Pull off the stove and oven knobs if possible and wash them in hot, soapy water. Clean beneath the knobs with an

24

old toothbrush, using baking soda as needed for additional scrubbing power.

3.   **Clean the oven:** If you have a self-cleaning option on your oven, by all means use it. After the cycle has ended and the oven cooled, wipe away any ash from the oven's walls and floor. If you don't have a self-cleaning oven, you can still get it clean without harsh chemical sprays — it's just going to be a longer process. Just be sure you do this on an UNHEATED oven.

- Sweep away piles of burned food then wash the walls and floor with hot, soapy water to remove as much grease as possible.
- For cooked-on stains, sprinkle baking soda and mist it with warm white vinegar; allow that to sit for a few hours then scrub the grime away.
- To remove baked grease from the oven door window, scrub it with a thick paste of baking soda and lemon juice. Allow that to sit for an hour then wipe clean.

4.   **Clean the microwave:** Heat a cup filled with equal parts water and white vinegar for 2 minutes. Don't like vinegar? Use a several lemon wedges, instead. Let the cup sit in the microwave for 2 more minutes while the steam loosens grime. Remove the turntable and wash it in the sink. Wipe the food splatters away with a damp microfiber cloth, and use a toothbrush if needed to clean the corners.

5.   **Shine them all:** For stainless steel appliances, use a dab of olive oil on a microfiber cloth to remove fingerprints and leave a nice gleam. Give other types of surfaces a nice shine using the All-Purpose Cleaner recipe in the "Homemade Cleaning Mixes" section of this book.

Today's Organizing Task: Glasses Cupboard

Over the year, many of us accumulate plastic glasses and water bottles, novelty cups, even coffee mugs. At first they seem like things we should hold onto, and then comes the day when you can't find matching glasses for a dinner party, and the ones you do find smell awful. It's time to do something about that.

1.   **Empty and wipe:** Empty the cupboard completely. Wipe the interior with a microfiber cloth dipped in warm, soapy water. Follow with another cloth dipped in clean, warm water, and allow to air dry.

2.   **Toss the trash:** Discard (or recycle) any chipped glasses, along with any drinkware you no longer want to keep. Keep in mind that if you have glass cupboard doors or open shelving, mismatched glasses make your kitchen look cluttered.

3.   **Soak and shine:** Deodorize and de-haze your drinking glasses by filling a sink with hot water and adding 2 cups of white vinegar. This works for both plastic and glass. Let the drinkware soak in this for 20-30 minutes while you work on the next step, and then rinse and dry. The vinegar will remove both the smell and the haze.

4.   **Scour stains:** Remove gray silverware scratches and stains from coffee mugs and tea cups by scrubbing with a paste of cream of tartar and water. Rinse well and dry.

5.   **Store them properly:** Return glasses to the cupboard, storing glasses of the same size together. If you have open shelving, store glasses upside down to keep them from accumulating dust. For those with young children, consider putting smaller glasses on the lowest shelf to make it easier for them to find. Less frequently used glasses, and those reserved for company dinners, should go on the top shelf.

Today's Maintenance Task: Daily Cleaning (Emphasis on Living Room)

As you're doing the Daily Cleaning Routine, spend some extra time on the living room for its weekly cleaning:

- Dust artwork, lamp shades, shelves and TV with a lightly dampened microfiber cloth. Rinse repeatedly so you're not simply spreading dust.

- Polish glass surfaces. Wipe down light switches, door knobs, and door jambs, too.
- Using the crevice attachment, vacuum around the base of walls, and then vacuum the floor.
- Polish the furniture.
- Empty the trashcan.

DAY SIX

The general rule is to clean from the outside in, and then from top to bottom, left to right. By cleaning the cupboards, drawers, and appliances, we've deep-cleaned the perimeter of the kitchen. Now it's time to give the rest of it a top-to-bottom cleaning.

Today's Cleaning Task: Finish the Kitchen

1.   **Empty the sink:** If there are dishes in your sink, wash them and then fill the sink with hot, soapy water. Use this on the following cleaning steps.

2.   **Let the light shine:** It is impossible to clean well in a dimly lit room. Open the blinds and turn on all of the lights so you can see every splatter and spot.

3.   **Cut the clutter:** For five days you've been doing the Daily Cleaning Routine, corralling the clutter on your kitchen counters and returning it every day to its proper place. As a result, today it should only take a moment to declutter your counters, so do it now.

4.   **Get dusting:** Using a long-handled cleaner or a broom with a pillow case slipped over the bristles, dust the ceiling and then the walls, window sills, door jambs, doors, and baseboards.

5.   **Clean cupboard and cabinets:** Grab a step stool or ladder and clear the top of your cupboards. Wash the tops and then the fronts of your upper cupboards using a microfiber cloth, rinsing it frequently. Repeat with the lower cupboards and the kitchen island.

6.   **Wipe before returning:** Dust items before returning them to the top of your cupboards.

7.   **Wash the windows:** Use a clean, dry microfiber cloth and some glass cleaner to polish the windows, the front of pictures on the walls, and other decorative glass surfaces. Note: if the sun hits your kitchen windows directly, wait until sunset to polish them or you'll just leave streaks.

8.   **Clear the counters:** Remove everything from your countertops and wash the back-splash with hot, soapy water. Rinse, dry and follow with glass cleaner for a nice shine.

9.   **Now, clean them:** Use hot soapy water to remove grease from the countertops and buff dry.

10.   **Wipe before returning:** Wipe small appliances, canisters, and other items as you return them to the counter.

11.   **Make it shine:** Spray appliance fronts with all-purpose cleaner and wipe them top to bottom to remove grime. For stainless steel appliances, use a small dab of olive or vegetable oil on a lint free cloth to remove fingerprints. Also spray and wipe light switch plates, doors (including the knob) and finally baseboards.

12.   **Scrub the sink:** Drain the sink and scrub it with baking soda to remove food stains. Clean the garbage disposal by filling it with a handful of ice and a sprinkling of baking soda then run it for 30 seconds with the tap wide open. To repel water spots, dry the sink with a towel and then buff it with a drop or two of olive or lemon oil.

13.   **Finish with the floor:** Sweep or vacuum the floor it using your machine's floor attachment. Be sure to move furniture and other items off the floor so you can get all of the dust and grit. Follow by mopping

the floor well with a floor cleaner and allow it to dry. (See "Homemade Cleaning Mixes.")

Today's Organizing Task: Silverware Drawer

Wipe your silverware drawer organizer to remove any crumbs then give your utensils a quick inspection. Use plastic bread ties to keep chopsticks or plastic utensils together so they don't take over your drawer.

> *Bonus tip: Items that have accidentally gone into the garbage disposal may have jagged edges -- smooth them with a nail file if possible, otherwise toss them before someone gets hurt.*

Today's Maintenance Task: Daily Cleaning and Laundry

In addition to the Daily Cleaning Routine, it's time to get caught up on laundry again. Keep in mind that we're washing sheets on the days we clean the bedrooms, and towels on the days we clean bathrooms. So today's laundry is just our family's clothes, and hopefully won't be too overwhelming.

Sort it, wash and dry it, then take it out of the dryer right away and fold it. Most importantly, *put away each load as soon as it's folded*. Putting away each load right away means your house still looks tidy even if you have to stop before you've finished all the laundry.

DAY SEVEN

Do you despise cleaning the bathroom? You're not alone. I've spent more time coming up with excuses to avoid cleaning the bathroom than it would have taken me to actually do it. But, let's face it: these rooms get nasty and they need to be cleaned well regularly.

Over the next few days we'll break into small steps the process of deep-cleaning these important rooms so our weekly cleanings will go that much faster. Note that if you have more than one bathroom, you'll need to do today's cleaning and organizing tasks in each.

Today's Cleaning Task: Bathroom Walls and Baseboards

Lots of things build up on bathroom walls. Wash yours using warm water to which you've added a few drops of dishwashing detergent. Work with a cleaning cloth that is damp but not dripping wet, and clean from the bottom up to avoid streaks.

- If hairspray buildup is a problem, do a second pass with one of these solutions:

    o *On painted walls:* Combine 1 part fabric softener and 2 parts warm water in a spray bottle.

    o *On wallpaper:* Use equal parts of rubbing alcohol and water in a spray bottle. Be sure to spot test first!

- Once you've cleaned the walls, wipe the baseboards with different microfiber cloth dipped in hot, soapy water then follow with a clean wet cloth.

Today's Organizing Task: Under Bathroom Sinks

1.   **Empty it:** Remove everything from beneath your bathroom sink. Since a lot of dust accumulates here, it's a good idea to wipe it first with a dry cloth to get the dry grime out of the way. Next, clean the interior of the cupboard with hot, soapy water and follow with a fresh cloth dipped in plain water.

2.   **Sort it:** Grab a trash bag and a box for donations, and go through the clutter underneath your bathroom sink. Throw away expired products, but consider donating unused items to your local women's shelter.

3.   **Group it:** Gather items you use daily into a basket so they're easy to find. Be sure to place these in the *front* so you don't have to rummage around looking for them. Use additional baskets, or even shoe boxes to group other items together — lotions and oils, for example, or all the items you use to polish your nails.

4.   **Raise it:** If space is at a premium in your bathroom, think about installing a multi-shelf storage unit under the sink.

Today's Maintenance Task: Daily Cleaning (Emphasis on Bedrooms)

While doing the Daily Cleaning Routine, spend some extra time giving the bedrooms a surface cleaning. We'll get to a deep-cleaning later on. For now, the daily cleaning plus the steps below equal a weekly cleaning.

1.   **Dust and polish:** Start with the ceiling fan then dust and polish dressers and other hard furniture, wall art, and window sills.

2.   **Clean soft surfaces:** Use your vacuum's dust or drape attachment and vacuum the curtains or blinds. Switch to the upholstery attachment and vacuum chair seats, throw pillows, and dry clean-only bed linens.

3.   **Change the sheets:** Be sure to launder the used sheets today, rather than leaving them in the laundry room. Doing a room's wash the same day you clean the room will keep laundry from piling up.

4.   **Finally, the floor:** Use the crevice attachment at the base of the walls, and then vacuum the rest of the floor thoroughly.

DAY EIGHT

Let's keep the cleaning going in the bathrooms (sorry for the pun) by tackling the nastiness that builds up in our tubs and showers. Remember, if you have more than one bathroom, do the cleaning and organizing tasks in each today.

Today's Cleaning Task: Hard Water Spots and Soap Scum

1.   **Clean the shower head:** If possible, remove your shower head and soak it in a bowl filled with equal parts hot water and white vinegar. If you cannot remove the shower head, fill a zippered plastic bag with the same 1:1 mixture and then, using a rubber band, fasten the bag around the shower nozzle so the head is immersed in the liquid. Wait 30 minutes then scrub the shower head with an old toothbrush and reattach it (or dump the contents of the bag).

2.   **So long, soap scum:** Remove soap scum from built-in soap holders and shower walls using a good soap scum remover like the homemade one found in the "Homemade Cleaning Mixes" chapter.

3.   **Out, darn spots!** The soap scum remover does a good job of removing spots from shower walls and doors and nasty rings on bathtubs. For tough buildup on whirlpool jets or fixtures, try this:

- Fill tub to 2 inches above the highest jet with HOT water.
- Add 1/2 gallon white vinegar.
- Run the jets for 15 minutes then let sit for another 10.
- Drain the tub and refill with cold water, running 10 minutes.
- Drain the tub and wipe down with clean, soft cloth.

IMPORTANT NOTE: The homemade cleaning recipes in this book are safe to use together. DO NOT use them at the same time as commercial cleaners! DO NOT mix commercial cleaners with each other, either, or you may create toxic fumes that can cause serious lung, liver, and brain damage!

Today's Organizing Task: Medicine Cabinet

Despite their name, did you know that medicine cabinets may not be the best place to store medicine after all? The heat and humidity in our bathrooms may lessen the effectiveness of medications, plus there's the danger of kids getting into them. According to experts, it's better to store them in cool, dry place — preferably one with a lock.

Also important: checking expiration dates. While most medications remain effective well past the date noted on the bottle, after a couple of years things start to get iffy. As a general rule of thumb if it's important for the medication to work, and the bottle says it expired more than a year ago, replace it.

1.   **Empty it:** Remove everything from your medicine cabinet. If the shelves are removable, take them out, too.

2.   **Wipe it:** Using a microfiber cloth dipped in warm, soapy water, wipe the inside of the cabinet, including the back of the door. Follow with a cloth dipped in clean water. Wash removable shelves in a sink of warm, soapy water and rinse them.

3.   **Sort it:** Separate your cosmetics from your medicines, first aid supplies and other items.

4.   **Check it:** Go through each group (cosmetics, pills, etc.) and toss expired items. With regards to makeup, mascara should be replaced every 2-3 months; foundation is good for 1 year; and powders expire after 2-3 years.

5.   **Group it:** Store similar items together in your cabinet. Put the most frequently used items on the lower shelves, less-often used items up high.

Today's Maintenance Task: Daily Cleaning (Emphasis on Laundry Room)

Today after you do the daily cleaning routine, head to the laundry room and give the appliances a quick wipe down, dust the shelves, polish the inside of the window, and sweep the floor.

DAY NINE

If you have more than one bathroom, do the cleaning and organizing tasks in each today.

Today's Cleaning Task: Shower Curtains

Although less frustrating than glass, shower curtains can still get funky because they trap moisture, becoming breeding grounds for mold and mildew. Short of buying new ones every few months (and I know someone who does just that, which seems silly to me), what can you do to clean them? Put them in the washing machine!

1.   **Wash shower curtains one at a time:** Add a couple of washcloths or a hand towel to "scrub" the curtain as the cycle runs.

2.   **Add this:** Use your regular detergent, 1 cup of white vinegar and hot water for plastic curtains, warm for vinyl, and cold for fabric overlays.

3.   **Catch drips:** Spread a bath towel in front of your washer. When the cycle is complete, take the wet shower curtain out of the machine and put it on the towel.

4.   **Hang it:** Carry the towel-wrapped curtain to your bathroom and hang it back up. Open it fully so the curtain can drip dry.

5.   **Air it:** Turn your bathroom fan on to help the curtain dry faster and to keep humidity from building up in your bathroom and causing mold or mildew.

34

Today's Organizing Task: Linen Closet/Shelves

Many of us need to store towels and washcloths in our bathrooms, while others are lucky enough to have separate linen closets. Wherever you keep yours, today's the day to get them neat and tidy.

1.	**Empty it:** Remove all of the towels, washcloths and other linens from where you store them.

2.	**Wipe it:** Using a damp microfiber cloth, wipe down the interior of the cupboard or closet. Be sure to get in the corners where spiders love to build webs. Allow to fully air dry while you continue with the next steps.

3.	**Sort it:** Group items together: towels, wash cloths, sheets, etc. For those who keep separate linens for guests, consider storing them on their own shelves so your family doesn't accidentally use (and stain) your nice stuff.

4.	**Inspect it:** While sorting, look through your linens and decide if anything needs to be mended or replaced.

5.	**Store it**: Ideally, you should change washcloths daily, towels after every three uses, and bed sheets weekly. Keep that in mind when returning your linens to the shelves and place the less-frequently changed items on higher shelves. To keep sheet sets neat, fold then slip them into one of the set's pillowcases. You'll be able to tell which bed it goes on, and your sheets won't fall all over the place.

Today's Maintenance Task: Daily Cleaning (Emphasis on Living Room)

As you're doing the Daily Cleaning Routine, spend some extra time on the living room. In addition to the daily tasks the following will give the room its weekly cleaning:

1.   Vacuum the curtains using the vacuum's dust attachment.

2.   Dust artwork, lamp shades, shelves and TV.

3.   Polish glass surfaces. Wipe down light switches and door jambs, too.

4.   Vacuum under sofa and chair cushions then vacuum the cushions themselves using the upholstery attachment.

5.   Using the crevice attachment, vacuum around the base of walls.

6.   Vacuum the floor.

7.   Polish the furniture.

8.   Empty the trashcan.

DAY TEN

We're continuing in the bathrooms today. If you have more than one bathroom, be sure to repeat these steps in each.

Today's Cleaning Task: Bathroom Grout

Grout. The word sounds as distasteful as the task of cleaning it, and yet it needs to be done. To clean yours naturally make a paste with baking soda and hydrogen peroxide then scrub it onto your grout using an old toothbrush. Wait 10-15 minutes and then rinse with hot water.

For tougher grout stains, make the paste out of Oxyclean and water and follow the directions above.

Today's Organizing Task: Hair Accessories

1.   **Brushes and combs:** If you haven't given your hair brushes and combs a good cleaning lately, this is the perfect time.

- Use scissors to snip between rows of bristles then run a comb through the bristles to remove hair.
- Fill a sink with warm water; add a squirt of dish soap, a couple tablespoons of baking soda, and a drop or two of tea tree oil (optional).
- Swish brushes and combs around in the water to remove oils and product buildup then rinse in clear water and lay flat on a towel to dry.

2.   **Styling tools:** Use rubbing alcohol on cool instruments to remove hairspray and product buildup. Either wrap the cords around the tools and store them in a drawer, or consider installing a styling tool holder inside a cupboard door.

3.   **Accessories:** The drawer inserts you'd use to hold silverware are also handy in the bathroom. Use one to organize barrettes, bobby pins, and hair clips. Or, if you have the shelf space, slip ponytail holders and scrunchies over the necks of decorative bottles.

Today's Maintenance Task: Daily Cleaning (Do family laundry)

Be sure to do your Daily Cleaning Routine then catch up on family laundry. (You'll be washing bathroom linens tomorrow.)

DAY ELEVEN

You have been deep-cleaning the bathrooms in small steps all week. Now it's time to wrap things up. Again, if you have more than one bathroom you'll want to do today's tasks in each.

Today's Cleaning Task: Deep-Cleaning Bathrooms

1.   **Look up:** Did you know dirty bathroom fans can cause house fires? These hard-working fans operate in rooms full of humidity, so they can easily become covered with dust, mold, and other grime. Grab a step-stool and remove the covers from your fans. Use a brush attachment on your vacuum to remove as much gunk as possible then give the blades a good wipe with a disinfecting spray. Be sure they're completely dry before replacing the cover.

2.   **Dust it:** Even bathrooms get dusty, particularly the light fixtures. Grab a long-handled duster, or a broom with a pillow case slipped over the bristles, and clean the ceiling and walls, including the corners. Move on to windowsills, door jambs, light fixtures and mirrors. Then, even though we wiped them clean earlier this week, give the baseboards a quick dust because we've just stirred up dust that might settle on them.

3.   **Shine it:** Turn the lights off and let them cool before completing this step! Grab a microfiber cloth and some glass cleaner. Remove light covers if necessary, and wipe both the bulbs and the light covers clean. (You can put the light covers in the top rack of your dishwasher if they're glass.) Let the glass cleaner fully evaporate before turning on the lights.

4.   **Disinfect it:** Spray the toilet inside and out with disinfecting spray. Allow it to sit several minutes while you move on to the next step.

5.   **Pre-clean then clean:** Clear the bathroom vanity, and then wipe it with a dry cloth. Repeat with the tub surround and the exterior of the toilet tank. These areas build up all sorts of dust and grime, so I've always found it easiest to dry wipe them first to remove that stuff, and *then* spray them with cleaner. Follow with a clean microfiber cloth, leaving the toilet tank for last, and your surfaces should be nice and shiny.

6. **Scrub then flush:** Grab your toilet brush and scrub the toilet bowl, taking extra care to get beneath the rim in the front where urine often collects and causes odor-producing stains. Flush then swish the brush in the clean water before flushing a second time. Prop the brush between the lid and seat to let it drip dry.

7. **Finish the floor:** Sweep or vacuum the floors and mop them thoroughly.

8. **Finish up:** Give the mirrors a good polish using glass cleaner then shine the faucet fixtures, change the towels and take out the trash. Be sure to wash your towels and any bathroom rugs TODAY so you don't fall behind on laundry!

Today's Organizing Task: Items on Your Vanity

Before returning items to your vanity, discard anything you no longer use. Return items that belong elsewhere to their appropriate spots. Then wipe down any items you'll be storing on the vanity.

Today's Maintenance Task: Daily Cleaning (Emphasis on Kitchen)

We deep-cleaned the kitchen last week, and now we're going to keep it looking nice by giving it extra attention during the Daily Cleaning Routine.

1. **Clean the main surfaces:** Wipe kitchen cupboard and drawer fronts with a clean microfiber cloth. Dust horizontal surfaces, including the top of the refrigerator. Wipe the kitchen table and chairs. Use furniture polish to give them a shine.

2. **Give the appliances the once-over:** Wipe away any spills on the floor of the oven. Go through the fridge and discard expired food items. Wipe the shelves with a clean microfiber cloth dipped in water. Wipe appliance exteriors. Scrub the sink.

3. **Polish the glass:** Use glass cleaner to shine fixtures and remove spots on the inside of windows. Polish the front of pictures, too.

4. **Take out the trash:** Empty the trash can and, if weather permits, rinse the cans outside then air dry.

5. **Clean the floor:** Clear the floor and then sweep or vacuum. Mop the floor and allow it to dry before returning items to their place.

DAY TWELVE

We've finished the bathrooms, so it's time to move on to another place that can make our mornings and evenings much more pleasant: the clothing closets!

Since cleaning the closet is a complicated task, there's a chart after the checklist for your reference. I *strongly encourage* you to read through the checklist to understand each step, even if you plan to use the chart.

Like bathrooms, you'll need to repeat these steps for *each*. One of the nice things about using a chart: you can hand it to your kids so they can clean their own closets!

Today's Cleaning AND Organizing Task: Clothing Closets

1. **Straighten what's there:** Throw away trash; gather clean clothes. Take dirty clothes to the laundry room. Fold and put away clean clothes that belong in the dresser and hang the rest.

2.   **Remove everything from the closet:** Take everything out of your closet and put it on your bed or floor. As you do, put "like" things together: pants, long-sleeved shirts, dresses, etc. Don't worry whether something's outdated or too big/small at this point.

3.   **Clean the empty closet:** Grab a long-handled duster, or a broom with a pillow case slipped over the bristles, and clean the ceiling, walls, and door jamb. Wipe scuffs off the walls. Dust the light fixture then wipe the light switch and baseboards. Vacuum the floor then use the crevice attachment at the base of the walls.

4.   **Sort your stuff:** Go through each category of clothes, sorting items into one of the following categories:

- *Things too worn out to wear or to donate:* Old t-shirts and tights make great stuffing for floppy sofa cushions. Everything else goes in the rag bag or trash.
- *Things you don't like anymore:* Put them into a box and label it 'Donations'. Keep a list of things you're donating as you put them into the box. This will make it easier to calculate your charitable donation to deduct from your taxes.
- *Things you like but which don't fit right now:* Put these items into a box marked "Store" and write the sizes on the outside of the box. Next time your weight fluctuates you'll know where to start shopping.

5.   **Return things to the closet in categories:**

- Hang clothing by category: jeans, skirts, dresses, long-sleeved tops, short-sleeved tops, etc. Put longer items toward the end of your closet rod to leave room for shoes.
- Return shoes to the closet.
- Hang scarves over the bar of a clothes hanger. Loop belt buckles over another clothes hanger.
- Return your shoulder bags and purses to the closet, preferably on a shelf.

6.   **Finish up:**

- Put the box of items to donate in your car
- Take the boxes of things you'll be keeping to your storage area.
- Take empty hangers to the laundry room.
- Throw away the trash.

Today's Maintenance Task: Daily Cleaning Routine

Even though closet-cleaning is very hard work, be sure to perform the Daily Cleaning Routine today. If you've been good about doing it every day you'll only need to spend a few minutes on it, but you'll reap the reward by having a pleasant, clutter-free home to relax in tonight.

Closet Cleaning Routine

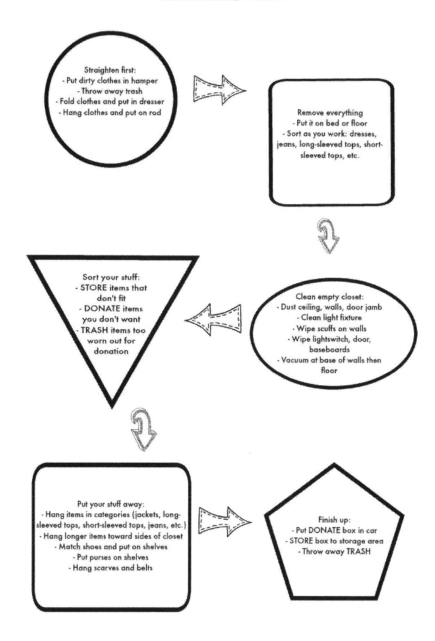

Straighten first:
- Put dirty clothes in hamper
- Throw away trash
- Fold clothes and put in dresser
- Hang clothes and put on rod

Remove everything
- Put it on bed or floor
- Sort as you work: dresses, jeans, long-sleeved tops, short-sleeved tops, etc.

Sort your stuff:
- STORE items that don't fit
- DONATE items you don't want
- TRASH items too worn out for donation

Clean empty closet:
- Dust ceiling, walls, door jamb
- Clean light fixture
- Wipe scuffs on walls
- Wipe lightswitch, door, baseboards
- Vacuum at base of walls then floor

Put your stuff away:
- Hang items in categories (jackets, long-sleeved tops, short-sleeved tops, jeans, etc.)
- Hang longer items toward sides of closet
- Match shoes and put on shelves
- Put purses on shelves
- Hang scarves and belts

Finish up:
- Put DONATE box in car
- STORE box to storage area
- Throw away TRASH

DAY THIRTEEN

"First impressions matter the most." This is absolutely true of our homes, too. You could spend all month cleaning but if the entrance to your home is a mess visitors are going to assume the rest is, too. Today you're going to put visitors on notice that there's been some serious organization and cleaning going on!

Today's Cleaning Task: Entry Way

Hopefully it's warm enough where you live to do some outside work. If not, you'll want to do the interior today and complete the exterior when you can.

Outside

1.   **Clear it:** Remove absolutely everything from your front step: the doormat, potted plants, knickknacks, etc.

2.   **Sweep it:** Grab a broom and sweep the walls, storm or screen door, front door, floor. Be sure to get the corners where leaves and cobwebs accumulate.

3.   **Scrub it:** Using a microfiber cloth and all-purpose cleaner, wipe your front door (including the frame of the storm- or screen door) to remove any grime, dust and fingerprints. Wipe the doorknob, door bell buttons, door knocker, kick plate and your house numbers, too.

4.   **Shine it:** Using a clean microfiber cloth and glass cleaner, shine the glass on your light fixtures inside and out. Clean glass on your storm or front doors.

5.   **Scour it:** If your front step is stained from plants or other decorative items, you'll want to scour the area with a stiff-bristled scrub brush. Mix up a quart of warm water and add 1/4 cup oxygenated

cleaner (like Oxyclean), and scrub this into the stain. Let it sit for 20-30 minutes then rinse with clean water. This non-toxic solution will remove mold, mildew and rust stains without harming your plants.

6.   **Shake it:** Shake or hose off your Welcome Mat before returning it to the front step.

7.   **Finish it:** Clean items as you return them to the front step. Remove dead leaves from plants, wipe down decorative objects, etc.

Inside

1.   **Clear it:** Gather shoes, coats, gloves and other items that belong in bedroom or coat closets and put them to their proper place. Collect items to be returned (library books, video rentals, etc.) and move them to your car so you can take care of them next time you're running errands.

2.   **Dust it:** Use a long-handled extension cleaner, or a broom with a pillow case slipped over the bristles, to dust the ceiling, walls, light fixtures, door jamb, door, and baseboards. Be sure to get in the corners to remove cobwebs!

3.   **Scrub it:** Use a microfiber cloth and all-purpose cleaner to remove scuffs and fingerprints from the door, trim and walls. Wipe the baseboards, too, and consider going over them with a dryer sheet to repel dust for up to two months.

4.   **Shine it:** Clean any light fixtures by hand using a microfiber cloth and glass cleaner. Shine doorknobs and other hardware.

5.   **Vacuum it:** Using a crevice attachment, vacuum around the base of the walls, and then use the floor attachment to get the floors clean. Vacuum both the front *and* back of throw rugs or entry mats, and then mop the floor.

6.   **Organize it:** Rather than merely tossing keys and cell phones wherever they land, consider using a decorative tray or bowl to corral them. Make space for a mail sorter, too. (More on that below.)

7.   **Protect it:** The entrance to your home is your last chance to keep dirt out. Studies indicate that shoes track in up to 70% of the dirt in a home, along with a number of pesticides. At a minimum, instruct your family to remove their shoes when they come in, and provide your guests a place to shed theirs if they like. If you can afford it and have the space, a basket with spare slippers or slipper socks can entice reluctant guests to shed their shoes. Also, be sure to have a good, dirt-catching mat *inside* your front door for everyone to wipe their feet.

Today's Organizing Task: Mail

Since we're cleaning the entryway today, it's time to do something about that huge pile of mail. You have probably read expert advice about using a mail-sorting system where you only touch items once. Sorry, but that doesn't work for me. I'm just not the type to drop what I'm doing and pay bills, sign permission slips, and write replies *that second,* nor do I know anyone who is.

A mail sorter, properly used, lets you open mail and file it for future action. I like one with four sections:

- *Read:* For things that aren't obviously bills.
- *Pay:* Bills.
- *Reply:* Letters or other things that need a response.
- *File:* This is where I stash paid bills along with receipts throughout the week. Once a week I file them in my home office.

Today's Maintenance Task: Daily Cleaning (Emphasis on Bedrooms)

While doing the Daily Cleaning Routine, spend some extra time giving the bedrooms a surface cleaning. We'll be giving them a deep-cleaning

46

very soon. Doing the daily cleaning plus the steps below gives them a weekly cleaning and will ultimately make the deep-cleaning go much faster.

- **Dust and polish:** Start with the ceiling fan then dust and polish dressers and other hard furniture, wall art, and window sills.
- **See to soft surfaces:** Use your vacuum's dust or drape attachment and vacuum the curtains or blinds. Switch to the upholstery attachment and vacuum chair seats, throw pillows, and dry clean-only bed linens.
- **Change the sheets:** Be sure to launder the used sheets today, rather than leaving them in the laundry room. Doing a room's wash the same day you clean the room will keep laundry from piling up.
- **Finally, the floor:** Use the crevice attachment at the base of the walls then vacuum the rest of the floor thoroughly.

DAY FOURTEEN

We're cleaning the laundry room this week, and since you've been doing family laundry weekly and each room's laundry on the day you've cleaned it, you shouldn't have mounds of dirty things to step around. If not, get that laundry done first!

Today's Cleaning Task: Washing Machine

Did you know that every pair of underwear has about 1/10th a gram of poop in it, and that after washing a load of them your machine contains E. coli? Nasty, right?

Even if you're washing in very hot water, using bleach or not, dead skin cells and other residues build up in your machine over time. Eventually, this stuff gets on your clothes.

Cleaning your machine regularly addresses both problems.

Top Loaders

1.   Open the lid and spray it then use a soft brush to remove any caked-on detergent or grime. Be sure to get the hinges, too.

2.   Using a microfiber cloth dipped in hot water, go around the hard rubber gasket at the top of the barrel. Scrub until you've removed any build-up then wipe down with a clean, wet cloth.

3.   Remove the bleach/fabric softener dispensers, if any, and scrub them in the sink using hot water and a soft-bristled brush. Dry well, and return to the machine.

4.   Run the wash cycle on the hottest water setting without detergent. Add 2 cups of white vinegar as the tub fills. Allow the cycle to run through its entirety, including rinse, to clean and disinfect the interior.

High-Efficiency Machines

1.   Use a soft-bristled brush and soapy water to clean the rubber gaskets around the door. Wipe with a clean, damp cloth and dry well.

2.   If your washer has a cleaning cycle, use it. Skip the detergent and instead fill the soap dispenser with white vinegar. Allow a complete cycle to run.

3.   If your machine does not have a cleaning cycle, add 2 cups white vinegar to the wash cycle (no soap) and run it on the HOT/HOT setting through a complete cycle.

Bonus Tip: You can reduce build-up and laundry odors by timing your loads of laundry properly. Wash clothing first, and follow it with a load that requires high-temperatures (sheets, towels, underwear and socks). Add bleach OR vinegar to the hot cycle and your machine will stay clean.

Today's Organizing Task: Laundry Room Shelves

You've done two general cleanings in the laundry room thus far. Now it's time to get serious about what you're keeping on the shelves.

1.   **Clear it:** Remove everything from your laundry room shelves. Toss trash into a bag as you work.

2.   **Dust it:** Clean the wall behind the shelves as well as the top and bottom of each shelf. (Yes, lint clings to the bottom.) Be sure to get the corners where cobwebs and lint accumulate.

3.   **Wipe it:** Grab a microfiber cloth and an all-purpose cleaner then wipe the shelves, including the wall behind them.

4.   **Group it:** Sort that pile of stuff you removed from the shelves by task: detergents; stain removers; other cleaning supplies; etc. Check for duplicates and consolidate them if possible. (Do NOT combine different products in the same container!)

5.   **Purge it:** Discard items you've discovered don't work well along with things you know you'll never use again.

6.   **Gather it:** Ordinarily, I'm not a big fan of shoving things in baskets but I make an exception in the laundry room where they're perfect for clothespins, batteries, extra laundry supplies, etc. Take the time to wipe things down as you transfer them to baskets or boxes so you aren't just dragging lint and dust from one place to another.

7.   **Return it:** Put your most commonly-used items (like detergents) at eye-level and save the higher shelves for things you don't use very often. Do NOT place dangerous items on shelves that

children can reach. This includes laundry detergent pods which little ones often mistake for candy.

Today's Maintenance Task: Daily Cleaning (Emphasis on Bathrooms)

Give the bathrooms a bit of extra attention today as you do the Daily Cleaning Routine. These steps, combined with those listed in the daily routine, amount to a weekly bathroom cleaning:

- Clean the sinks, including the faucets.
- Disinfect then scrub the toilet bowl.
- Wipe the exterior of the toilet.
- Remove hard water spots on the fixtures or shower walls.
- Clean the tub.
- Dust the door jambs and baseboards.
- Sweep or vacuum then mop the floor.
- Empty the trash.

DAY FIFTEEN

It's back to the laundry room today for a task too many homeowners ignore: dryer maintenance.

Today's Cleaning Task: Dryer

According to the National Fire Protection Association, there were over 15,000 house fires caused by dirty clothes dryers in 2010. Regular maintenance can reduce your fire risk while also improving your dryer's efficiency. Here's how:

1.   **Clean the exterior:** Dryers build up a lot of lint and dust on the outside. Wipe yours clean with a dry microfiber cloth to remove lint before spraying on your favorite cleaner and wiping it clean with a different cloth.

2.   **Clean the drum:** Using an all-purpose cleaner, wipe down the inside of the dryer drum. Be sure to look for and remove any threads, pieces of tap, or other items stuck in the fins of older-modeled dryers.

3.   **Clean the interior:**

- First, unplug the dryer. If it's gas-operated shut off the gas, too.
- Pull out the lint trap and clean it using hot, soapy water and a soft-bristled brush. Rinse until the water freely flows through the screen. Do not return it to the dryer until it's completely dried.
- With the lint screen removed, use your vacuum cleaner crevice attachment to clean as far as you can into the lint trap.
- Pull the dryer away from the wall as far as the vent tubing allows (usually about 2 feet). Slide the vent off then reach into the hole on the back of the dryer and pull out all of the lint you can find. If your vacuum can reach, use that.
- Every two to three years you should unscrew and remove the back of the dryer so you can vacuum away any lint that's built up. It will surprise you how much collects there!
- With the vent tubing still off, reach into the tubing itself and pull out any lint you can find. A vacuum works nicely on this part, too.
- Look through the vent hole that goes through the wall to the outside of the house. Vacuum if you can reach it or use your hand and a sturdy cloth to remove any lint buildup.
- Sweep then mop the floor beneath your dryer.
- Reconnect the vent tubing to the exterior vent and to the back of the dryer.
- Push the dryer back in place, and plug it in. (Gas dryers: turn the gas back on.)

Today's Organizing Task: Bookshelves

Some of my very favorite people reside within the covers of books. As an avid reader, I'm constantly adding books to my shelves, and that means I'm constantly adding shelves to my home. One thing I've learned from collecting books that I didn't learn from reading them: books are dust magnets. That's why it's important to clean your shelves regularly.

1.   **Peruse it:** Look at your shelves and remove things that don't belong there, like books that belong to someone else or your kids' toys. Give both back to their owners.

2.   **Purge it:** Sometimes you know you'll never re-read a book. Rather than throwing them in the trash (the horror!) set your unwanted books free so someone else can enjoy them. Bookcrossing.com makes it fun to do this, or you can turn used books into cash by trading them in at Amazon.

3.   **Organize it:** I like to keep my fiction separate from non-fiction, which I break down into cookbooks, history books, reference books, etc. Fiction gets sorted into literature, fantasy, historical fiction, etc. I'm not so picky that I get alphabetical by title or author but, hey, if you've got time…

4.   **Clean it:** Remove all of the books from a shelf, dust the shelf, and then dust each book as you return it to its place.

5.   **Wipe it:** Clean the exterior of your shelf with a damp cloth to remove dust and then polish it. Take care not to spray furniture polish on the books themselves.

Today's Maintenance Task: Daily Cleaning (Catch Up on Laundry)

After you've done your Daily Cleaning Routine, take time to catch up on laundry. All caught up? Then put your feet up and enjoy being at the halfway point of this 30-Day Cleaning and Organizing Plan!

DAY SIXTEEN

Today's Cleaning Task: Finish Laundry Room

1.   **Dust it:** Dust the ceiling, walls, window sills, windows, door jambs, doors and baseboards. Go over the machines and shelves one more time, too, since you've just stirred up a lot of gunk.

2.   **Scrub it:** Using a microfiber cloth and all-purpose cleaner, remove greasy fingerprints and scuffs from the walls and doors. Give the baseboards a quick spray and wipe, and then use a dryer sheet to wipe the baseboard and repel dust and lint for up to two months.

3.   **Polish it:** Use some glass cleaner and a clean microfiber cloth to polish the window and any metal hardware.

4.   **Vacuum it:** Vacuum the floor with the floor attachment. Be sure to get in the corners where lint accumulates.

5.   **Mop it:** Use a mop or microfiber cloth and floor cleaner to give the floor a good cleaning and leave it with a nice shine.

Today's Organizing Task: CDs, DVDs and Games in the Family Room

We've finished deep-cleaning the laundry room, so now it's time to begin the process of deep-cleaning the family and/or living room. Let's start that by tackling the entertainment cabinet first.

1.   **Clear the shelves:** Pull all of your CDs, DVDs, and games from the shelves where you keep them in the family room.

2.   **Wipe it:** Use a damp microfiber cloth to wipe the shelves thoroughly, both above and below. (Yes, dust accumulates on the bottom of things.) If your shelves are wood, now's a good time to use some furniture polish to give them a nice shine.

3.   **Organize it:** Alphabetize your DVDs and CDs. Divide your games by console (PS4, Wii, XBox, etc.) then alphabetize each group, too.

4.   **Purge it:** If your kids have outgrown certain games or movies, consider selling them to Amazon or listing them on eBay. Places like Goodwill might welcome them, too.

5.   **Shelve it:** Return the remaining items to shelves by group. As you do, take a moment to make sure titles all face the same way; they'll be easier to find and they'll look better, too.

Today's Maintenance Task: Daily Cleaning (Emphasis on Cupboards)

We've cleaned and organized a number of cupboards already. Today as you do your Daily Cleaning Routine, take a moment to straighten each of these cupboards again so they stay nice:

- Under kitchen sink
- Kitchen food storage container cupboard
- Bathroom cupboards and medicine cabinet

DAY SEVENTEEN

Family and living rooms often have a lot of wood in them. If you've got small children, pets, or a rowdy teenager like mine, your furniture probably takes a beating throughout the year. Rather than live with those nicks and gouges, we're going to do something about them.

Note: If your home has both a family and living room, you'll want to complete today's tasks in each.

54

Today's Cleaning Task: Wood Furniture in the Family/Living Room

1.   **Remove wax buildup:** Mix 1/2 cup warm white vinegar and 1/2 cup warm water in a shallow bowl. Apply in the direction of the wood grain using a clean, lint-free cloth. (Fabric baby diapers and microfiber cloths are perfect for this.) Immediately rinse with another clean cloth dipped in water. Buff dry using a third dry cloth.

2.   **Remove oil stains:** Stir 1 scoop oxygenated cleaner into 1 cup warm water. Dip a corner of a cleaning cloth into this mix and get the oil stain wet. Do NOT saturate the wood or you'll just create a water stain. Now take a soft-bristled toothbrush and work the cleaner into the stain, using additional small amounts of solution, until the stain is gone.

3.   **Disguise scratches:** Light scratches can be hidden by rubbing nut meat (walnut, pecan, etc.) along the scratch. The oil from the nut will darken the scratched wood, making it unnoticeable. Other options: coffee grounds for dark wood; iodine for mahogany; ashes for black wood; and shoe polish or markers for anything in between. For deeper scratches, use a matching Crayon or a kit from the hardware store.

They're small steps, and easy tasks to perform, but they really can make a big difference in how our furniture looks. I don't know about you, but little things like that can make or break my mood when I'm tired and stressed.

Today's Organizing Task: Coat Closet

Get your days off to a good start by taming the clutter in this important spot!

1.   **Empty it:** Pull everything out of the closet.

2.   **Dust it:** Clean the ceiling, walls, shelves, rack and baseboards. Be sure to get the corners where cobwebs tend to grow.

3.   **Wipe it:** Using a clean microfiber cloth and some all-purpose spray, wipe down the closet rod, the inside of the door and door jamb, and finally the baseboards. Consider rubbing a dryer sheet over the baseboard to repel dust and lint for up to two months.

> *Bonus Tip: Run a piece of wax paper over the closet rod so hangers slide more easily.*

4.   **Vacuum it:** Use the floor attachment to vacuum the closet floor.

5.   **Clean it:** Mop using a good floor cleaner and allow it to dry.

6.   **Purge it:** Go through the items you've pulled out of the coat closet and purge outgrown clothing items. Put them in a box marked "Donations" and stick them in your car so they don't just hang around. Return clothes that belong in other rooms and then return what's left to the closet.

7.   **Organize it:** Consider adding an over-the-door shoe holder to corral smaller items like mittens, hats, even spare keys.

8.   **Box it:** If your family leaves their shoes in the coat closet like mine does, consider adding a plastic box to hold their shoes. This is a habit I started a while back, and it never fails to amaze me how much dirt accumulates in the bottom of that box every week. But, hey, that's dirt that's not in my carpets, and it's easy to tip it into the garbage can!

9.   **Dehumidify it:** If your coat closet tends to smell musty, stash an open box of chalk inside (even kids' sidewalk chalk will work) to absorb moisture and prevent mildew.

Today's Maintenance Task: Daily Cleaning (Emphasis on Kitchen)

You've already deep-cleaned the kitchen, so now it's important to maintain your accomplishment. As part of the Daily Cleaning Routine, complete the following in the kitchen, too:

- Clean cupboard and drawer fronts.

- Wipe spills on the oven floor.
- Wipe the ceiling fan blades.
- Scrub the sink.
- Shine fixtures and remove spots on the inside of windows.
- Dust the top of cupboards, the top of the refrigerator, and other horizontal surfaces.
- Purge expired food from the fridge and quickly wipe down the shelves.
- Clean the kitchen table and chairs then shine them with furniture polish.
- Empty the trash can.
- Sweep or vacuum and then mop the floor.
- Change the towel.

Note: Today is a good time to head to your local charity to drop off the Donation boxes in your car.

DAY EIGHTEEN

As one of the most-used rooms in our homes, the Family (or Living) Room takes a lot of time and effort to deep-clean. So today you'll be doing both your cleaning and organizing tasks in this room, rather than spreading your attention throughout the house.

Today's Cleaning Task: Family/Living Room Blinds and Curtains

The second dustiest place in a room isn't the furniture, it's the window coverings. (The floor is the dustiest, in case you were curious.) If you've got blinds, you've probably seen how the dust builds up. Did you know there's usually plenty of grease on blinds attracting that dust?

If you use curtains, too, they're collecting dust as well. Let's do something about that today.

Vinyl or Plastic Blinds

1.   **Fill it:** There is no easier place to clean blinds than in the bathtub. Fill yours with 2 inches of water then add 2 cups of white vinegar and 1 tablespoon non-moisturizing liquid dish soap. (Original Dawn works best). Swirl that around so everything mixes together, but don't create foam.

2.   **Bathe them:** Pull each set of blinds all the way up, remove it from the window, and carry it to the bathroom. Release the blinds so they're fully open then lower them into the tub to soak for 10-20 minutes. (You can do two sets of blinds at a time.) Drain the tub, run the shower to rinse them off, and then hang them over the shower curtain rod to drop-dry. Be sure to place a towel beneath them to catch the drips.

3.   **No bathtub? No problem:** If you don't have a tub to soak the blinds, you can put them in the bottom of your shower. Fill a spray bottle with 1 cup hot water, 1/4 cup white vinegar, and 3 drops non-moisturizing liquid dish soap. Spray the blinds until they are soaking wet. Let them sit 10-20 minutes before running the water to rinse them, then hang them over the shower rod to dry.

4.   **Dry them:** Allow the blinds to dry thoroughly before returning them to place. If you're in a hurry, you can use a blow dryer -- just be sure you don't stand on a wet floor while you work.

5.   **Shine on:** Before re-hanging your blinds, wipe down the inside of the window sills and clean the windows with glass cleaner and a microfiber cloth. Hang the blinds and proceed to the next set.

Curtains

1.   **Remove them:** Take the curtains off the rods. Dust the rods.

2.   **Shine on:** Wipe the inside of the window sills and clean the windows with a glass cleaner and microfiber cloth.

3.   **Spin them:** If your curtains are washable, follow the instructions on the manufacturer's tag to launder them and remove dust. Dry clean-only curtains can be tumbled in the dryer for 10 minutes with NO HEAT to remove dust.

4.   **Hang them:** Remove curtains from the dryer and hang them immediately. If you're prompt about it, your curtains will be wrinkle free.

Today's Organizing Task: Purging Subscriptions

Let's take the plunge and move old magazines and newspapers (do people actually read paper newspapers anymore?) to the recycling center. If you're worried about missing something essential, scan the table of contents, find the articles you must have, and pull them out. Staple those "must read" articles together then put them in that mail sorter you set up on Day Thirteen and read them *tonight*.

Today's Maintenance Task: Daily Cleaning (Emphasis on Tub/Shower)

We splashed around in the bathroom while cleaning blinds today. After finishing the Daily Cleaning Routine, take some time to mop up drips, clean the tub and shower, and give the fixtures a good shine.

DAY NINETEEN

We're once again focusing both cleaning and organizing tasks on the family room. Again, if you have a formal living room, a lounge or other sitting area, perform today's tasks in each.

Today's Cleaning Task: Family Room Ceiling, Walls, Baseboards and Art

Ceilings collect a surprising amount of dust, especially textured or "popcorn" ceilings like the ones in my home. Every time you open the windows or run the fan, that dust gets stirred up and showers down on your furniture and floors. Let's get rid of that dust today.

1.   **Clear the walls:** Remove all wall decor and place it on the sofa or floor, then cover with a sheet to catch dust.

2.   **Clean the ceilings:** An extension cleaning kit makes this task much easier. A long-handled duster, a broom with a pillow case slipped over its bristles, or even a foam paint roller do an excellent job of cleaning both popcorn and flat ceilings.

3.   **Clean the walls:** Dust the walls, door jambs and window frames from top to bottom, paying careful attention to the corners where cobwebs accumulate. (In my house cobwebs are only visible when we have company.)

4.   **Clean the baseboards:** Use the duster on the baseboards.

5.   **Wipe things down:** Before returning your wall decor to place, wipe each item with a lightly damp microfiber cloth to remove dust. Polish the glass on photos and pictures using a microfiber cloth and glass cleaner, and shine wood frames with a lint-free cloth and furniture polish. Be sure to get the backs, too!

Today's Organizing Task: Items That Belong Elsewhere

Now it's time to get rid of items that are hanging out in the family or living rooms but belong elsewhere. (Don't get distracted by purging things you don't like anymore; we'll get to that.) Rather than work at this willy-nilly, it's much faster and far more effective if you get methodical.

1.   **Grab it:** Find a laundry basket or bag to hold items.

2. **Work the room:** Stand at the door, facing toward the room. Work from your left and continue all the way around the room until you're back at the door.

3. **Be a detective:** As you work, look on shelves, in drawers, under furniture, etc. When you find items that belong elsewhere, put them in the basket or bag.

4. **Sort it:** Once you've made your way through the whole room, take the items to your kitchen table. Take items out of the basket or bag one at a time, placing them in groups according to the room where they belong.

5. **Return it:** Return groups of items to their appropriate location.

Today's Maintenance Task: Daily Cleaning (Emphasis on Bedrooms)

While doing the Daily Cleaning Routine spend some extra time working in the bedrooms. We'll be focusing on them next week, but they're due for a weekly cleaning. The following steps will accomplish that *and* make next week's cleaning a bit easier.

1. **Dust and polish:** Start with the ceiling fan then dust and polish dressers and other hard furniture and window sills.

2. **See to soft surfaces:** Use your vacuum's dust or brush attachment to clean the curtains or blinds. Switch to the upholstery attachment and vacuum chair seats, throw pillows, and dry clean-only bed linens.

3. **Change the sheets:** Be sure to launder the used sheets today rather than leaving them in the laundry room. Doing a room's wash the same day you clean the room will keep laundry from piling up.

4. **Finally, the floor:** Use the crevice attachment at the base of the walls then vacuum the rest of the floor.

DAY TWENTY

If you have a family room and a formal living room, lounge or sitting room, you'll need to perform today's cleaning and organizing tasks in *both*.

Today's Cleaning Task: Smudges and Fingerprints

Rumor has it that some people actually enjoy repainting their walls, changing their color based on Pantone's color of the year or just on a whim. I'm not one of them. I spend a *lot* of time cleaning smudges off my walls, doors and windowsills to keep our interior paint looking nice. Here's how.

Greasy fingerprints: All-purpose cleaner won't work and might ruin the paint finish. Instead, grab a piece of white chalk (the kind teachers use on blackboards) and gently rub it on the greasy fingerprints. Let this sit for 5 minutes while the chalk dust bonds to and absorbs the oils in the fingerprint. Wipe the chalk away with a dry microfiber cloth, then a damp cloth to remove any residue. No chalk? No problem. Dab at the spots with a piece of white bread.

Crayons: Make a paste of baking soda and water, and lightly rub it on the mark with a clean white cloth. (Do NOT do this on high gloss walls — use WD-40 sprayed on a clean white cloth instead.) Rearrange the cloth in your hand frequently so you're constantly working with a clean surface, rather than rubbing crayon dye back onto the walls. When the marks are gone, wipe the area with a lightly damp microfiber cloth.

Permanent marker: Wet a cotton ball with rubbing alcohol and dab at the spot. Switch cotton balls frequently and repeat until it's gone. Follow with a lightly damp microfiber cloth.

Pencil marks: Use a pencil eraser. If the mark remains, follow the directions for removing crayon marks above.

Scuffs: Again, a pencil eraser may do the trick. Otherwise, Mr. Clean Magic Erasers do a brilliant job of removing scuffs from matte finishes. For high gloss finishes, spray some WD-40 on a clean white cloth and wipe the scuff away.

Today's Organizing Task: Purge Unwanted Items

Yesterday you purged subscriptions. Today it's time to purge more: throw away broken items. Then, gather other things you no longer enjoy or find useless and box them up for donation. Don't forget to put that box in your car so you can take it to your local Goodwill or other charity!

Today's Maintenance Task: Catch up on laundry

After completing the Daily Cleaning Routine, it's time to catch up on your family's laundry. Please remember the rule about doing laundry: fold and put it each load away as soon as it's out of the dryer!

DAY TWENTY-ONE

Again, if you have a family room and a living room, sitting room or lounge, you need to complete these tasks in each.

Today's Cleaning Task: Furniture and Carpet Stains

Carpet stains: Most stains come up easily when sprayed with 1 cup warm water and 1 tsp. non-moisturizing liquid dish detergent. Don't saturate the carpet or you'll get the pad wet, and that can lead to mold problems. Use a clean, white cloth to dab at the stain with the idea of transferring it from the carpet to the cloth. Rotate the cloth as you work so you're constantly working with a clean spot. Once the spot is lifted, dab the area again with a clean, damp cloth without using soap, then put a dry towel on top and stand on it to lift away any remaining moisture.

Microfiber furniture: Microfiber is the easiest furniture fabric to clean. A good rub with a baby wipe can often get stains out of this fabric, but for tougher tasks try a drop or two of dishwasher detergent on a damp microfiber cloth. Be sure to wipe it clean with a detergent-free cloth once the stain is gone.

Ink stains: Lightly dampen a clean, white, lint-free cloth with rubbing alcohol and dab at the stain. Be sure to change out the area of cloth you're working with so you're constantly lifting the ink out of the furniture and transferring it to your cloth. Once the stain is gone, wipe the area with a microfiber cloth dampened with clear water.

Food stains: Scrape off as much of the mess as you can then make a paste of equal parts water and baking soda. Stir in 2 drops of liquid dish soap. Use an old toothbrush to work this into the stain and allow it to sit for 5 minutes. Scrape the residue away and wipe the area with a wet microfiber cloth repeatedly to remove the paste. Allow the area to dry and repeat if needed.

Grease stains: Sprinkle with cornstarch and work the powder in thoroughly with an old toothbrush. Allow this to sit for 5 minutes or so then vacuum until the cornstarch is gone. Treat the remainder of the stain following the steps listed above for food stains.

Today's Organizing Task: Blankets, Throws, and Pillows

Launder all of your blankets and throws following manufacturer instructions. Store those that are out-of-season in your linen closet or empty suitcases in the closet.

Be sure to launder <u>all</u> of your throw blankets regularly. They're odor and allergen magnets, so wash them at least every other week at the hottest setting appropriate for their fabric.

Pillows can often be laundered in the washing machine, too. Check the label and follow its instructions. For washable pillows, launder two at a time to keep the load balanced, and add a tennis ball to the dryer to fluff the pillows as they tumble. Or hang them by a corner on a line and let the sun do the work.

Today's Maintenance Task: Daily Cleaning (Emphasis on Laundry Room)

After the Daily Cleaning Routine, spend some extra time giving your laundry room the once-over:

- **Wipe it:** Wipe the exterior of the washer and dryer.
- **Dust it:** Dust your laundry room shelves, doorjamb, window sills and baseboard.
- **Polish it:** Clean spots off window interiors and glass surfaces using a microfiber cloth and glass cleaner.
- **Scrub it:** Using a microfiber cloth and an all-purpose cleaner, get rid of any fingerprints or smudges on the walls, door and trim.
- **Vacuum it:** Use the floor attachment to clean the floor.
- **Mop it:** Finally, mop the floor and empty the wastebasket.

<u>Note</u>: today is a good day to take the Donation boxes in your car to your local charity!

DAY TWENTY-TWO

If you have a family room and a formal living room, lounge or sitting room, you'll need to perform today's cleaning and organizing tasks in each.

Today's Cleaning Task: Finish Family/Living Room

1.   **Wipe it:** Grab a wet microfiber cloth and wipe your baseboards.

2.   **Dust it:** Start at the room's entrance and work your way clockwise around the room, dusting everything (and *under* everything!), from high to low. Use a damp microfiber cloth and rinse it frequently.

3.   **Polish it:** Use a lint-free cloth and furniture polish on wood furniture and decorative items.

4.   **Shine it:** Get glass surfaces gleaming with a dry microfiber cloth and glass cleaner.

5.   **Clean it:** Remove pillows from sofas and chairs and, using your vacuum's upholstery attachment, vacuum the furniture thoroughly. Return the pillows to place.

6.   **Move it:** Move small furniture from where it ordinarily sits and vacuum beneath. Be sure to get help for this if you have back problems!

7.   **Vacuum it:** Go around the base of the walls using the vacuum's crevice attachment. Follow this by vacuuming the rest of the room, using attachments as needed to get under heavier furniture.

Today's Organizing Task: Back to the Bathroom

You've already deep-cleaned the bathroom cupboards, but it's important to revisit that area regularly so they stay neat. Go through the cupboards and drawers in all of your bathrooms and set things straight. Since you've done this recently, it won't take more than a few minutes but it will prevent clutter and disorganization from creeping back.

Today's Maintenance Task: Daily Cleaning

You did quite a bit of work in the family/living room(s), so when you're finished with the Daily Cleaning Routine it's time to kick back on the sofa and enjoy what you have done!

DAY TWENTY-THREE

This week, we are focusing on bedrooms which can be overwhelming when you're truly deep-cleaning. Again, I've broken the process down into simple steps that build on each other day after day. As always, repeat the day's steps in each bedroom. If you can't get them all done today that is fine: this isn't a competition!

Today's Cleaning Task: Bedroom Ceilings, Walls and Baseboards

Clean, dust-free air in the bedroom is essential for allergy and asthma sufferers. Even if you don't suffer from those conditions, clearing the dust out of your room can make for a much better night's sleep.

1.   **Clear the walls:** Cover the bed with a sheet or several towels. Remove artwork and other decor from the walls and place them on the covering.

2.   **Cover up:** Lay a second clean sheet or blanket over the artwork on the bed. Be sure this covers your pillows and blanket or duvet so you don't get it dusty, too.

3.   **Fans first:** If you have a ceiling fan, now is the time to clean it. Stand on a stepstool and carefully slide a pillowcase over each blade, letting the dust fall into the pillowcase. Or use an extension cleaning kit with a ceiling fan attachment.

4.   **Ceilings second:** Use a long-handled duster, a broom with a pillow case slipped over the bristles, or even a paint roller. You'll be surprised at how much dust comes down. Be sure to focus on the area around your ceiling fan, which tends to collect a lot of dirt, as well as where the walls and ceilings meet.

5.   **Move on down:** Move on to dusting the walls and then the baseboards, in that order.

6.   **Hang it:** Carefully gather up the covering laid over the artwork. Set it aside. Wipe each piece of artwork or decor with a lightly damp microfiber cloth and return it to the wall. Don't forget to get the backs of pictures: it's amazing how much dust collects there, too! Shine the glass fronts of pictures with a clean microfiber cloth and glass cleaning spray. (See "Homemade Cleaning Mixes")

7.   **Shake it:** Gather up the coverings you'd used to protect your bed and artwork from dust. If you have more than one bedroom to clean, take the coverings outside and shake away any dust as you transition from one bedroom to the next. Launder the coverings when you've cleaned the final bedroom.

Today's Organizing Task: Purging Clutter

If your bedroom has been basically doubling as a storage/junk room, or if you're cleaning your teen's room, you've got your work cut out for you.

1.   **Prepare it:** You need three boxes or trash bags. Don't even think about using just one or making piles. You need THREE boxes or trash bags!

2.   **Label it:** With masking tape and/or a marker, label one bag/box TRASH, the second DONATE, and the third RETURN.

3.   **Trash it:** Grab the container you've labeled TRASH and, starting to the left of the door, pick up all trash or items too broken/gross to be used ever again. Work your way completely around

the room. Don't open drawers; we'll get to those another day. Toss magazines, newspapers, food wrappers, etc. Set that bag outside the bedroom door.

4.　　**Gather it:** Repeat this process with the DONATE box. Be ruthlessly honest with yourself as you work. That pile of clothes on the floor that you tried on but didn't fit? You can't wear them but someone else can. Donate them. Be just as honest outgrown toys, books you'll never re-read, decor you no longer like, etc. Put this box in the back of your car.

5.　　**Grab it:** Do one more pass through the room, this time with the box you've labeled RETURN. Grab anything that belongs in another room. Did your child leave a toy on your dresser? What about the DVD you watched in bed but need to put back in the family room? Again, leave what's in the drawers for later this week.

6.　　**Return it:** Take the RETURN box of items to the kitchen table. Sort them based on where they belong so you don't have to make several trips to the same room. Return those items to their proper places.

7.　　**Repeat it:** Now, repeat this same process in every bedroom you'll be cleaning. By the time you're done, your dressers, nightstands and floors should be looking *much* neater. That's good — it'll make cleaning them easier later this week!

Today's Maintenance Task: Daily Cleaning (and Laundry)

After you do the Daily Cleaning Routine, it's time to catch up on your family's laundry. This is the time to launder those piles of clothes you picked up from your bedroom floor, along with anything else in your hamper. Be sure to fold and put away each load as soon as it's done in the dryer!

DAY TWENTY-FOUR

It's back to the bedrooms today to tackle more areas that collect dust and debris. Remember, although I've tried to keep the steps small enough that you can repeat them in each bedrooms, it's *perfectly fine* if you spend more than one day to do these steps -- don't burn yourself out!

Today's Cleaning Task: Curtains/Blinds and Windows

Window coverings collect a surprising amount of dust, and then scatter it throughout the room when you open them in the morning and close them at night. Rather than starting and ending your day in a cloud of dust, let's do something about it by following the cleaning steps for blinds, curtains, and windows listed on Day Eighteen.

Today's Organizing Task: Nightstand

Nightstands are places to hold items we need in bed. For some reason, mine seems to accumulate all sorts of other things, too: hair ties, cough medicines, wrappers from an entire box of candy bars I bought for my son's school fundraiser and won't share. (Don't judge me.) It's time to do something about that mess.

1.   **Toss the trash:** Grab a bag of some kind and collect all the TRASH on your nightstand. Look under it, too. Now, open the drawers and toss any crumpled tissues, old magazines, half-eaten candy bars, etc.

2.   **Donate the unwanted:** This time, go through the items on and in the nightstand and gather anything you want to DONATE to charity. That book you read but will never read again? Toss it in. What about that alarm clock that you stopped using when you bought your smartphone? Add it to the box, too. Keep going until you've gathered

everything that's still useable and in good shape but you no longer want to hold onto. Put the box in your car to take to your local charity.

3.   **Return the clutter:** Now, gather everything that you need to RETURN to where it belongs. Do you *really* want your nail polish in your nightstand? What about those cough medicines from the last time you were sick -- shouldn't they go into the locked medicine cabinet? Put things that belong elsewhere into the bag and take them to your kitchen table. Sort them by where they should go, and return them to their proper place.

4.   **Dump it:** Spread a towel on the bed and dump what's left in your nightstand drawers on the towel.

5.   **Wipe it:** Clean inside each drawer with a lightly damp microfiber cloth, including on the dust that collects in the corners.

6.   **Reset it:** Put away the items you'll be keeping in your nightstand. As you work, keep in mind that your top drawer should contain items you're likely to need most often: tissues, hand lotion, the remote control, etc. The bottom drawer(s) are suitable for things you don't need frequently, like candy bars. (I said, *don't judge!*)

Today's Maintenance Task: Daily Cleaning (Emphasis on Bathrooms)

Give the bathrooms a bit of extra attention today as you do the Daily Cleaning Routine. These steps, combined with those listed in the daily routine, amount to a weekly bathroom cleaning:

- Disinfect and scrub the toilet bowl.
- Wipe the exterior of the toilet.
- Remove hard water spots on the fixtures or shower walls.
- Clean the tub and shower.
- Dust the door jambs and baseboards.
- Sweep or vacuum then mop the floor.
- Empty the trash.
- Set out clean towels and wash the dirty ones.

DAY TWENTY-FIVE

Considering how much time we spend in bed (roughly one-third of our lives), shouldn't our beds be welcoming places of calm and comfort? By the end of today your bed will be just that.

Today's Cleaning Task: Beds, Mattresses and Bedding

You've seen the commercials warning about a mattress doubling in weight over the course of eight years due to dust mites, sweat and dander (also known as your dead skin). They aren't exaggerating: a used mattress can have up to 10 million dust mites in it.

And what do dust mites feed on? Dead skin cells, of which you shed 30,000 to 40,000 *every hour*. In addition to the roughly 230,000 to 320,000 you'll shed in an average night's sleep, your body is also exuding sweat… and where do you think that sweat goes? That's right: straight into your mattress!

The bad news: there's no way to really get rid of those things. The good news: we can at least reduce the colonies on the surface, while also freshening our mattress and ensuring a better night's sleep. Here's how.

1.   **Strip it:** Remove everything from the bed: sheets, blankets, duvets, pillows, dust ruffles, mattress pads and covers.

2.   **Wash it:** It's important to launder your bedding on the hottest setting the fabric can handle. High temps, both in the washer and dryer, kill dust mites and other allergens. For efficiency's sake, launder in the following order:

- Mattress pad/cover
- Pillows — Two per load. Add tennis balls or clean sneakers to the dryer cycle to fluff them.
- Sheets and pillowcases
- Blankets

- Duvets, comforters, bedspreads and dust ruffles. (Check the label to ensure they can be machine washed! If not, tumble them in the dryer on a LOW or NO HEAT setting for 10-15 minutes to dislodge dust.)

3.   **Dust it:** Using a lightly damp microfiber cloth, wipe your headboard, bed frame, and the legs of your bed. Rinse the cloth repeatedly as you work so you're not spreading dust.

4.   **Sprinkle it:** While the bed is bare, sprinkle the mattress well with a cup of baking soda and rub that in with a stiff-bristled brush. Wait 10 minutes and then, using the upholstery attachment, vacuum the top and sides of your mattress thoroughly first in a horizontal then a vertical direction.

5.   **Clean it:** Remove stains from your mattress as follows:

- *Dried Blood Stains:* Treat with a solution of 1/4 cup hydrogen peroxide mixed with 1 tbsp. *each* liquid dish soap and table salt. Rub this into the stain and allow it to sit until dry before scraping the residue off. Dab at any remaining stain with a white rag dipped into hydrogen peroxide, rotating the rag as the stain lifts off. (Using a white rag prevents dye transfer from the cloth to the mattress.)

- *Urine Stains:* Dissolve 3 tbsp. baking soda in 8 oz. of hydrogen peroxide then add a drop or two of liquid dish soap. Dab that solution on to the spot. (Do NOT drench your mattress!) Meanwhile, whisk together 3 parts dry laundry detergent powder and 1 part water to make a dry foam. Rub that into the stain (which should still be damp from the first step) and let it sit for 30 minutes. Scrape away any residue and vacuum.

6.   **Flip it:** If you have a mattress that can be flipped over, do so once any treated areas have completely dried. Get assistance if you need it, and then repeat the steps above.

7.   **Move it:** While your bed is bare, and if you have the strength to do it, move the bed and vacuum beneath it. If you're unable to move your bed, use your vacuum's floor attachment to clean beneath it.

8.   **Make it:** As each load of bedding is finished drying, remove it from the dryer immediately and return it to the bed.

Today's Organizing Task: Dressers

Yesterday, you tackled the nightstand. Today it's time to take on the dressers. As always, the first step is to grab three bags/boxes/laundry hampers and label them: TRASH, DONATE, and RETURN.

1.   **Clear the surface:** Remove everything from the top of dressers, tossing trash and items that belong elsewhere. Look at what remains and determine if you want to keep or donate it.

2.   **Work methodically:** Rather than dump your dresser's contents on your freshly cleaned bed, work one drawer at a time starting at the top. This also ensures that the room isn't torn apart should you get interrupted. (It happens.) Go through each drawer in three passes:

- *Discard trash:* Toss food wrappers, tissues, scraps of paper, etc. Also toss clothing that is too stained or torn to be donated. (Or recycle those items by stuffing them into floppy throw pillows.)
- *Cull for charity:* Be ruthlessly honest with yourself about the clothes in your dresser. Donate items that you haven't worn in over a year to charity. Do the same with items that no longer fit (or create a fourth box marked STORE and fill it).
- *Move it:* It's common for things to wind up in our dresser that have no business there. Those spare buttons some clothing manufacturers include with garments are best kept in a Mason jar or pretty container. Receipts should be filed in your home office. Whatever is in your dresser that doesn't belong there goes into the RETURN box.

3.   **Wipe it:** Wipe the empty drawer with a damp microfiber cloth to remove any dust and debris.

4. **Fold it:** Neatly fold items before returning them to the drawer. You may find some things, like underwear, take up less space when rolled. The important part is to group like items together in a drawer.

5. **Move on:** Repeat this process until you've gone through the entire dresser.

6. **Finish it:** Dump the TRASH box into the garbage can. Place the DONATE box in your car. If you created one, move the STORE box to your storage area. Then take the RETURN box to the kitchen table and sort its contents based on where items belong. Take each room's items back at the same time so you aren't making a bunch of unnecessary trips.

Today's Maintenance Task: Daily Cleaning (Emphasis on Family/Living Room)

We've already deep-cleaned these rooms, so while doing the Daily Cleaning Routine we're going to stay on top of what we've accomplished.

- *Dust and polish:* Start with the ceiling fan then dust tables, shelves, other hard furniture and window sills. Dust artwork on walls and knickknacks on tables. (Dust beneath them, too!) Use a lint-free cloth and furniture polish to give wood furniture a nice shine.
- *See to soft surfaces:* Use your vacuum's dust or drape attachment and vacuum the curtains or blinds. Switch to the upholstery attachment and vacuum chair seats, throw pillows. Lift cushions and vacuum beneath them. Vacuum the arms of sofas and chairs, too.
- *Finally, the floor:* Use the crevice attachment at the base of the walls then vacuum the rest of the floor thoroughly.

DAY TWENTY-SIX

You've done a lot of work in the bedrooms this week. Now it's time to finish up. As always, complete these steps in each bedroom, taking as many days as you need.

Today's Cleaning Task: Finish Bedroom Cleaning

1.   **Clean the lights:** Use a clean microfiber cloth to dust non-fabric lampshades. Fabric shades are most easily cleaned with a lint roller. Be sure to clean both the outside and the inside of the shade. Turn the light off, let the bulb cool, then spray some glass cleaner on a clean microfiber cloth and wipe the light bulb to remove any dust and grime.

2.   **Baseboards:** Use a damp microfiber cloth to wipe the baseboards. If you have fabric softener sheets, rubbing the baseboards will help repel dust and pet hair.

3.   **Hard stuff:** Remove any sticky buildup on your wood furniture. Now is a good time to cover any scratches in your wood furniture, too. (See "*Day Seventeen*" for directions on both.)

4.   **Soft stuff:** Use the upholstery attachment on your vacuum cleaner to remove dust from throw pillows, soft upholstery and stuffed animals.

5.   **Floor time:** Start by using the crevice attachment to vacuum the floor where it meets the walls. A *lot* of dust builds up here, even on hard floors. Once you've gone around the base of all walls, thoroughly vacuum the floor. Move small furniture and vacuum beneath it, getting assistance if needed.

6.   **Toss it:** Empty the trash can and wash it using 1 cup hot water, 1/2 cup white vinegar and a stiff scrub brush. Rinse well and let air dry.

> *Bonus Tip: Keep your trashcan clean by lining it with a plastic grocery bag, or put a paper towel on the bottom.*

Today's Organizing Task: Items on Stairs

In many homes, including mine, stairs act like temporary shelves holding things that need to be taken up on future trips. Don't even think about cleaning *around* that stuff.

1.   **Put it away:** Grab a laundry hamper, put everything on the stairs in it, and carry it to where it belongs.

2.   **Dust it:** With a dusting attachment on an extension cleaning pole, dust the ceiling above the stairs, the walls, and the baseboards.

3.   **Wipe it:** Using a microfiber cloth and all-purpose cleaner, wipe the banisters, walls, and baseboards to remove fingerprints and grime. If you have stairs with hard flooring, use a lightly damped microfiber cloth to clean them.

4.   **Vacuum it:** Vacuuming carpeted stairs requires a bit of patience. It's not enough to vacuum the treads (where your feet step) -- you also need to vacuum the risers (where you stub your toes) because dust collects there. Start by using the crevice attachment to vacuum the carpet where it meets the baseboards, and then vacuum the crevice at the base of each step. Switch to the upholstery attachment (I've found this one works best) and vacuum each tread then the riser below it, continuing from the bottom step to the top.

Today's Maintenance Task: Daily Cleaning (and Laundry)

You've done a lot of work today but don't skip the Daily Cleaning Routine. Catch up on family laundry when you're done. Today is also a good day to take the Donation boxes in the back of your car to your local charity.

DAY TWENTY-SEVEN

Not every home has a dining room. If yours doesn't, skip to the maintenance part of today's tasks and enjoy the chance to catch your breath!

Today's Cleaning Task: Dining Room

1.   **Clear it:** In many homes the dining table is buried under months of clutter because it's such a convenient place for homework and storage. If this is true of yours, the first step is to clear it. You'll need two containers marked TRASH and DONATE.

- *Toss it:* Go through the mess on your dining table and pick out the trash. This includes food wrappers, old magazines, broken toys, etc. Put them in the box marked TRASH and set it aside.
- *Donate it:* Go through the remaining pile on your dining table and be ruthlessly honest about what's left. Toys, DVDs, magazines and other items that have been there for longer than you can remember really aren't part of your life. Put them in the DONATE box and take that box to your car.
- *Gather it:* Whatever is left — aside from table linens — belongs somewhere else. Don't dither about this: there's no reason your dining table should hold anything besides dining-related items! Group them on the table based on the room where they belong then take them to their proper place. Continue until your table is clear.

2.   **Protect it:** Spread thick towels over your cleared dining table to protect its surface.

3.   **Clear the walls:** Take artwork and decor off the walls and place it on the towels.

4.   **Clear the windows:** Refer to the steps listed on Day Twenty-Four to clean blinds, curtains, and windows.

5.   **Let it shine:** With the windows bare it's time to grab a microfiber cloth and glass cleaner to give them a nice shine. Do the same for hanging light fixtures and sconces. IMPORTANT: Be sure light bulbs are cool when you clean them.

6.   **Dust it:** Use a long-handled duster to clean:

- Ceiling, including recessed lights
- Window trim, sashes and sills
- Doors and door jambs
- Walls (especially in corners and where they meet the ceiling, since cobwebs accumulate there)
- Baseboards

7.   **Wipe it:** Clean marks on walls using the steps listed on Day Twenty.

8.   **Hang the artwork:** Use another damp microfiber cloth to wipe artwork and decor before returning it to the walls. Make sure you wipe the back of items, too — a lot of dust accumulates there. Remove the towels from your dining table and set them aside.

9.   **Polish it:** Now's a good time to remove sticky wax buildup and repair scratches in dining furniture. (You'll find directions to doing both on Day Seventeen.) Then use a lint-free cloth and furniture polish to give your wood furniture a shine.

10.   **Vacuum it:** Using the crevice attachment, go around the base of your walls carefully. Switch to the upholstery attachment and vacuum chair cushions. Finally, pull the chairs out of the room and thoroughly vacuum the floor.

Today's Organizing Task: China Hutch/Breakfront

You should still have your TRASH and DONATE containers handy from the previous step.

1.   **Protect it:** Grab those towels you set aside in the previous step, and spread them on your table again.

2.   **Empty it:** Remove the contents of your china cabinet and set everything on top of the towels.

3.   **Wipe it:** Use a damp microfiber cloth to wipe the interior of your cabinet, including the back and the bottoms of the shelves.

4.   **Inspect it:** Take a look at your cabinet and repair any scratches in the wood. (See "Day Seventeen")

5.   **Polish it:** Use a lint-free cloth and furniture cleaner to shine the hutch. Use a clean microfiber cloth and glass cleaner to clean glass doors and fixtures.

6.   **Sort it:** Take a good, long look at the items on the table. Put broken items in the TRASH container. Be ruthless about the remaining items: are there some you no longer use? Put them in the DONATE box. As for things that belong in another room, group and return them to their proper rooms.

7.   **Refill it:** Return remaining items to the cabinet. It's a good idea to place frequently-used items to shelves that are waist- and eye-level. Less commonly used items should go on the top.

8.   **Wrap it up:** Dump the box labeled TRASH into the garbage can. Take the box marked DONATE to your car.

9.   **Reveal it:** Remove the towels you've been using to protect the table and put them in the wash.

10.   **Set it:** Spread a nice cloth on your dining table and top it with an attractive centerpiece. This protects your tabletop from scratches, but more importantly it sends your family a message that the dining table is no longer the place for clutter.

Today's Maintenance Task: Daily Cleaning (Emphasis on Kitchen)

As part of the Daily Cleaning Routine, spend some extra time on the kitchen to give it a weekly cleaning.

- Clean cupboard and drawer fronts.
- Wipe up spills on the oven floor.
- Wipe the ceiling fan blades.
- Scrub the sink.
- Shine fixtures and remove spots on the inside of windows.
- Dust the top of cupboards, the top of the refrigerator, and other horizontal surfaces.
- Purge expired food from the fridge and quickly wipe down the shelves.
- Clean the kitchen table and chairs. Shine them with furniture polish.
- Empty the trash can.
- Sweep or vacuum the floor using your vacuum's floor attachment.
- Mop the floor.
- Change the towel.

DAY TWENTY-EIGHT

You've cleaned the various rooms in our homes, so today it's time to clean the space connecting them.

Today's Cleaning Task: Hallways

1.   **Clear the walls:** Remove any artwork, photographs and other decor from the walls. Put it on the floor.

2.   **Look up:** Grab an extension pole cleaner if you need it, or a broom with a pillowcase slipped over the bristles, and dust the ceiling, including any recessed lights. Next, dust walls then baseboards.

3.   **Shine it:** Turn the lights off, and allow the bulbs to cool. Remove any light fixture coverings and wash them in the sink using hot, soapy water. Rinse and dry them. (If they're glass, you can run them through the dishwasher to save yourself the effort.) When the bulbs are cool, use a microfiber cloth and glass cleaner to remove dust and grime. Give them a few minutes to completely dry before turning the on the lights.

4.   **Clean it:** Hallway walls, doors, and door jambs tend to take a lot of abuse. Follow the steps listed on Day Twenty to clean marks and scuffs on your hallway walls.

5.   **Wipe it:** Using a clean, damp microfiber cloth, wipe the baseboards. Follow with a dryer sheet to repel dust.

6.   **Hang it:** Wipe the artwork, photographs, and other decor with a damp microfiber cloth before returning it to the walls. Be sure to get the backs where dust also collects.

7.   **Finally, the floor:** Use the crevice attachment and vacuum the floor at the base of the walls. Next vacuum the floor thoroughly. Since this is a high-traffic area, it's a good idea to vacuum once going along the length of the hall, and then in shorter strokes across the width of the space.

Today's Organizing Task: Home Office Paperwork

Filing paperwork is one of the most boring home organization tasks so it's no surprise we all tend to put it off until our home offices contain mounds of papers mingled with trash. Then comes the day we need to find one specific bill or receipt among the jumble and we panic, knowing it's like trying to find a needle in a haystack. Let's end that cycle.

1.   **Get ready:** Grab three boxes and label them FILE, SHRED, and TRASH.

2.   **Gather it:** Rake your papers into one huge pile. I know some organizational experts say you should only touch a paper once, filing it directly in the appropriate location. That method has never worked for me; I find it so slow that I usually give up and find something more entertaining to do. So we're going to use my method instead.

3.   **Start at the top:** Beginning with the top of your pile, go through each paper and decide what needs to be done with it.

- FILE: If a paper pertains to tax deductions (see below); is something you want for future reference (like recipes you haven't yet tried); or is a keepsake (your child's straight-A report card), place it in the FILE box.
- SHRED: Papers no longer needed to support old tax returns (which should be kept for 7 years); those annoying credit card offers you don't want; and other papers with identifying information (names, addresses, email addresses, etc.) belong in the SHRED box.
- TRASH: Everything else goes in the trash box. As with all organizing tasks, it's important you are *ruthless* about this!
- Set aside the SHRED and TRASH boxes when you've made the first pass through your pile.

4.   **Sort it:** Going through the contents of the file box, pick up each individual paper and decide what kind of file it should go into. Sort papers into stacks based on the kind of file they'll need. Here are some ideas:

- *Family keepsakes:* Create a file for each family member to hold their mementos.
- *Recipes to try:* Just what it says.
- *Tax-related documents:*

  ☐   Income: Pay stubs, W-2s, 1099s, interest statements, dividend statements. Also include jury duty pay.

  ☐   Medical expenses: Receipts from doctors, dentists, hospitals, labs, pharmacies, vision centers, etc. Also receipts for any payments made to purchase health, dental, and vision insurance.

☐ Charitable donations: Include receipts for cash donations, as well as donated items (clothes, toys, etc.).

☐ Real estate papers: Year-end mortgage interest statements, real estate tax documents, home owner's insurance receipts, and other paperwork associated with casualty losses to your home. If you made home improvements, include their receipts here. They may/may not be tax deductible (talk to your financial advisor), but at least you'll know where they are.

☐ Property and sales tax papers: Receipts for paying taxes on cars and other vehicles subject to personal property tax. Also, sales receipts for big-ticket items.

☐ Child care payments: In addition to receipts from daycare, be sure you have paperwork with your babysitter's contact information and Social Security number if you paid him/her to watch your child while you worked or looked for work.

☐ Student loan payments: Any papers related to payments made and interest charged.

☐ Work-related expenses: Receipts for work-related expenses not reimbursed by your employer (e.g., work-related educational expenses, union dues, professional license renewal fees, tools or supplies required for your job, etc.)

☐ Self-employment expense receipts (if applicable): Receipts for advertising, office supplies and cleaning, office repairs, etc.

☐ Utility bills for home-office deduction (if applicable): If you qualify for a home-office deduction, you'll need your home's utility bills to calculate the amount deductible from your taxes.

- *Statements:* Statements from banks, credit cards, insurance companies, and other financial institutions all need individual files.
- *Warranties:* If you have the space, it's nice to have a separate file for each item you're keeping a warranty for. That way you can file not only the warranty but the instruction manual and any receipts associated with repairs. If you don't have the space then make one large file to hold all of your warranties together.

5.   **And so on:** It's better to have more files than fewer, even if they only hold one sheet of paper, *as long as you clearly label them.* The idea is being able to open the drawer and find what you're looking for immediately.

6.   **Safeguard the essentials:** Some things should never be in your home office files because they're too difficult to replace in the event of fire or other natural disaster. These items include birth and marriage certificates; passports; photocopies of your credit cards (front and back) and driver's license; stocks and bonds; and Wills. These should be stored in a fire-proof home safe — you can find one for as little as $30. Keep it in the basement of your home where it's less likely to be exposed to prolonged heat in the event of a house fire.

7.   **File it:** Once you've sorted your papers, file them! That seems like an obvious step but you'd be surprised how many people simply stop once they've got things sorted, hoping to come back later to do the filing. That's how unmanageable piles start.

8.   **Trash it:** Grab the box of paper marked TRASH and dump it in the garbage can. Do not even think about letting it sit around or you're not cleaning, you're hoarding.

9.   **Shred it:** You need a shredder for your home. They're not expensive, and if you keep one where you sort your mail you'll find it easy to shred unwanted mail as it comes in. If a shredder's not in your budget, check with your local office supply stores. Staples, Office Max and other stores offer shredding services, often for free. Make the call *today*, and get your stuff down there!

Today's Maintenance Task: Daily Cleaning (Emphasis on Laundry Room)

Do the Daily Cleaning Routine as usual then give the laundry room a little extra attention. Use a damp microfiber cloth to give the appliances a quick wipe down and dust the shelves. Finally, sweep and mop the floor and you're done.

DAY TWENTY-NINE

Now that you've dealt with the paperwork in your home office it's time to give this room a little extra TLC.

Today's Cleaning Task: Home office ceiling, walls, and baseboards

1.   **Cover up:** Lay a clean sheet or towels over your desk to protect the surface.

2.   **Clear the walls:** Remove artwork and other decor from the walls and place them on the desk.

3.   **Fans first:** If you have a ceiling fan, clean it. Carefully slide a pillowcase over each blade, letting the dust fall into the pillowcase, or use an extension cleaning kit with a ceiling fan attachment.

4.   **Ceilings second:** Carefully dust the ceiling. Focus on the area around the ceiling fan, where a lot of dust collects, as well as where the walls and ceilings meet.

5.   **Move on down:** Next, dust the walls and then the baseboards, in that order.

6.　　　**Hang it:** Wipe artwork, photos and other wall decor with a lightly damp microfiber cloth to remove dust before returning it to the walls. Shine the glass fronts of pictures with a clean microfiber cloth and glass cleaning spray. Don't forget to get the back of items, too, since dust collects even there.

Today's Organizing Task: Office Shelves

For the sake of efficiency, today's organizing task involves a bit of cleaning, too.

1.　　　**Clear it:** You should still have a sheet or towels on your desk, so remove everything from your office shelves and put it on the desk.

2.　　　**Dust it:** Use a dry microfiber cloth to dust the empty shelves, including the backs and bottoms of each shelf.

3.　　　**Wipe it:** With a lightly damp microfiber cloth, wipe the shelves down to remove grime and fingerprints.

4.　　　**Label it:** Grab three bags, boxes or laundry hampers. Label them TRASH, DONATE, and RETURN.

5.　　　**Sort it:** It's time to weed through the things that have accumulated on your shelves. As with all decluttering, you've got to be ruthless and realistic.

- *Trash it:* Old magazines you'll never get around to reading, items you've been meaning to repair but haven't had time for -- they're trash. Put them in the TRASH box/bag and let them go.
- *Donate it:* Maybe there are some books you once loved but won't read again? Knickknacks that no longer hold sentimental value for you might still make someone else smile. Put them in the DONATE box and take that down to your car.
- *Return it:* Things that have migrated to your home office shelves but belong elsewhere should go into the RETURN box. Once you've collected everything that belongs in a different room, set

this box outside the door of your home office. When you're finished today, you'll want to take things back to where they belong.

6.   **Shelve it:** Return what's left to your home office shelves, wiping each item with a dry microfiber cloth as you work. Place frequently-used items on the most easily-accessible shelves; heavy items belong on the lowest shelves; and things you rarely use should go on the highest shelves since you don't need to reach them very often.

Today's Maintenance Task: Daily Cleaning (Emphasis on Bathrooms)

As you do the Daily Cleaning Routine, spend some extra effort on the bathrooms to give them their weekly cleaning. The steps in the daily plan plus those below will cover it:

- Disinfect and scrub the toilet bowl.
- Spray the exterior of the toilet with disinfecting spray, allow it to soak for 2 minutes then wipe.
- Spray the shower walls and/or tub with disinfecting spray, allow it to soak for 2 minutes then wipe.
- Dust the door jambs and baseboards. Wipe away fingerprints.
- Sweep or vacuum then mop the floor.
- Empty the trash.
- Change the towels and launder the dirty ones.

DAY THIRTY

It's the final day! You have cleaned bathrooms and bedrooms, the laundry room and the kitchen. You've organized junk, spice, and cutlery drawers. You've kept your house tidy day in and day out using the Daily Cleaning Routine, and you've kept up with weekly cleanings throughout.

In other words, you are tired… but that's okay because you are also just about done.

Today's Cleaning Task: Office Curtains/Blinds, Windows and Floors

1.   **Window coverings:** Follow the steps listed on Day Eighteen to clean blinds, curtains, and windows.

2.   **Finally, the floors:** Vacuum the floors at the base of the walls using the crevice attachment, then vacuum the rest of the floor. Remember, thorough vacuuming requires four passes (back and forth, back and forth) to get the dirt out, and high traffic areas need and additional four from a different angle.

Today's Maintenance Task: Daily Cleaning

Complete the Daily Cleaning and you are done! Well, okay, you are done for *today*, but that doesn't mean you can ignore your home tomorrow. The key to maintaining what you've accomplished is doing something *every day* so never gets out of control.

It's the regular, daily attention that tells our family that we want them to help keep the home clean. In sociology, this is known as the "broken window theory": if the first sign of disorder or disrepair is ignored (as in, a broken window), it's interpreted as a sign that standards won't be enforced. Before long the entire area falls into decline.

That doesn't mean you have to repeat the plan over and over. Instead, use the Monthly Cleaning Routine to keep chaos away. You can always refer back to the Plan when you want to -- say, for Spring Cleaning -- but if you keep up with the Monthly Cleaning Routine you'll probably find you don't need to.

Daily Cleaning Routine / Dining Room / Clean the Vacuum

Daily Cleaning Routine / Dining Room / Clean the Dishwasher

Daily Cleaning Routine / Dining Room / China Hutch

Daily Cleaning Routine / Dining Room / Clean the Dishwasher / Change Air Filter

Daily Cleaning Routine / Kitchen / Wash Towels / Clean Drains

Daily Cleaning Routine / Kitchen / Wash Towels / Clean Oven

Daily Cleaning Routine / Kitchen / Wash Towels / Top of Cupboards

Daily Cleaning Routine / Kitchen / Wash Towels / Straighten Cupboards

Daily Cleaning Routine / Living Room / Entry Way / Wash Rugs

Daily Cleaning Routine / Living Room / Entry Way

Daily Cleaning Routine / Living Room / Entry Way / Stair Rails

Daily Cleaning Routine / Living Room / Entry Way / Furniture Stains

Daily Cleaning Routine / Straighten: / - Pantry / - Junk Drawer

Daily Cleaning Routine / Linen Closet / Coat Closet

Daily Cleaning Routine / Clean Smudges: / - Walls / - Doors / - Windows

Daily Cleaning Routine / Home Office / File Papers

Daily Cleaning Routine / Clean Freezer / Bathrooms / Wash Towels

Daily Cleaning Routine / Med. Cabinets / Bathrooms / Wash Towels

Daily Cleaning Routine / Clean Freezer / Bathrooms / Wash Towels

Daily Cleaning Routine / Bathrooms / Wash Towels / Bookshelves

Daily Cleaning Routine / Clean Fridge / Bedrooms / Wash Sheets

Daily Cleaning Routine / Under Sinks / Bedrooms / Wash Sheets

Daily Cleaning Routine / Clean Fridge / Bedrooms / Wash Sheets

Daily Cleaning Routine / Bedrooms / Wash Sheets / Nightstand / Dresser

Daily Cleaning Routine / Spice Drawer / Wash Clothes

Daily Cleaning Routine / Laundry Room / Wash Clothes

Daily Cleaning Routine / Bedroom Closets / Wash Clothes

Daily Cleaning Routine / Laundry Room / Wash Clothes

HOMEMADE CLEANING MIXES

Indoor air pollution is a very real concern, particularly in newer homes which are built to prevent outdoor (fresh) air from seeping inside. Quite literally everything you cook or burn, spray or wipe, wash or clean with in your home becomes part of the air you breathe. For that reason, it's important to think about the products you use.

Bleach is a powerful cleaner, but it can also lead to lung and skin irritation. Other commercial cleaners do an excellent job of disinfecting but they, too, can leave harsh fumes lingering in the air. Even air fresheners contain potential irritants -- and they don't list ingredients, either!

By using homemade cleaning mixes you know if your family is allergic to any of the ingredients. They're also just as good at disinfecting, cleaning, and polishing. Even better, you probably already have the ingredients in your kitchen to make just about any cleaning product you need.

Bonus Tip: Use peppermint oil to scent your homemade cleaners and you'll deter cockroaches, mice and ants, too!

91

All-Purpose Cleaner

Thanks to the lemon and vinegar, this cleaner has light germ-killing properties. It also leaves a lovely scent and a nice, streak-free shine. Keep a bottle under the kitchen sink along with a microfiber cloth for quick touch-ups. Stash other bottles in the guest bathroom so you can tidy things if company drops in.

NOTE: Do not use the recipe above on granite or marble. Use the Granite-Safe All-Purpose Cleaner instead!

Ingredients:

2 cups warm water

1 tablespoon baking soda

1/2 cup white vinegar

Juice of one lemon

5-10 drops lemon essential oil

Directions:

1. In a bowl, stir the baking soda into the water dissolved.

2. Add the remaining ingredients *in order*. Stir well.

3. Transfer to a spray bottle.

4. Shake gently before each use.

Granite-Safe All-Purpose Cleaner

The acidic nature of my standard All-Purpose Cleaner can ruin granite countertops. Use this non-acid solution instead.

Ingredients:

1/2 cup isopropyl (rubbing) alcohol

1 1/2 cup water

1/4 tsp. liquid dish detergent

Essential oils (optional)

Directions:

1.   Combine the ingredients in a spray bottle.

2.   If using essential oils, add just enough to counteract the smell of the rubbing alcohol. (It will fade quickly after spraying, so the use of oils is purely optional.)

3.   Shake gently before each use.

4.   Rubbing alcohol is highly flammable so KEEP THIS AWAY FROM FLAMES! That includes gas stove burners, pilot lights, and candles.

Floor-Cleaner for All Hard Flooring

If you've been looking for a streak-free, inexpensive floor cleaner that cuts through grime without harming your floors, look no further. This works on linoleum, vinyl, ceramic and porcelain tiles. It ALSO works on laminate, engineered, and hardwood floors!

Again, since we're using rubbing alcohol, it's important that you keep it away from flames. So don't spray this near hot water heaters, lit burners, pilot lights or candles, please.

Ingredients:

1/2 cup white vinegar

1/2 cup Isopropyl (rubbing) alcohol

1/2 cup water

3-5 drops liquid non-moisturizing, non-oxygenated dish soap (for example, Ivory or Dawn Original)

5-10 drops essential oils (optional, see below)

Directions:

1.   Combine ingredients in order in a spray bottle and spray on your floor as you mop.

2.   To make a large amount of floor cleaner to use in a bucket, pour a bottle of Isopropyl (rubbing) alcohol into a clean bucket. Fill the bottle with white vinegar and add to the bucket. Fill the bottle again with water and add to the bucket. Add 1 teaspoon of Ivory or Dawn Original dish soap and 20-30 drops of your favorite essential oil (optional). Discard unused solution after cleaning.

Bathroom Disinfectant Spray

This spray relies on borax and washing soda, which is different than baking soda. You can find borax and washing soda in the laundry aisle of most big-box stores like Wal-Mart and Target. Both amplify the disinfecting power of white vinegar while helping the solution cling to surfaces a bit longer. For added disinfecting power, use tea tree or lavender essential oil.

Ingredients:

1 tsp Borax

1 tsp of washing soda

2 cups hot water

1/2 cup white vinegar

10-15 drops of essential oils

Directions:

1.   Using a funnel, pour the powders into a spray bottle.

2.   Add the hot water first and the vinegar second. (Otherwise it will bubble up.)

3.   Close the bottle and swirl very gently.

4.   Add the essential oils. Close the bottle again and swirl lightly before use.

Bathroom Disinfecting Scrub

In this recipe we're relying on essential oils to do the disinfecting. If you're still concerned about whether your surfaces are properly disinfected, follow with the Bathroom Disinfecting Spray above. Store any leftover scrub in an air-tight, opaque container for future use.

Ingredients:

1/2 cup baking soda

1/2 cup washing soda

1/2 cup liquid Castile soap

Essential oils: 10 drops lemon, 10 drops lavender, and 5 drops tea tree

Directions:

1.   In a small bowl, mix first three ingredients to form a paste.

2.   Stir in essential oils.

To use: sprinkle the paste on your damp sponge or the surface to be cleaned then scrub. Rinse with hot water.

Soft Scrubbing Cleaner

Ingredients:

3/4 cup baking soda

2 tbsp. liquid dish OR 1/4 cup Castile soap

2 tbsp. white vinegar

Hot water as needed

6-10 drops essential oils (optional)

Directions:

1.   Combine the baking soda and soap in a bowl to form a paste.

2.   Slowly stir in the vinegar (it will make a small fizz).

3.   Add hot water as needed to make a very thick paste.

4.   Add essential oils until you're happy with the fragrance.

5.   Transfer to an airtight, opaque container.

6.   To use: sprinkle on to damp microfiber cloth or sponge and scrub.

Soap Scum Remover

Ingredients:

Dawn or Sun Original dish soap

White vinegar heated until VERY hot

An empty spray bottle

Directions:

1.   Using a measuring cup, add equal parts VERY hot vinegar and dish soap to the spray bottle. Stir to combine but don't create a foam.

2.   Heavily spray the shower door or surface that you want to clean.

3.   Let sit 30 minutes to overnight.

4.   Spray with water or wipe clean with a microfiber cloth and warm water. Note: the shower floor will be slippery, so be careful!

5.   Scrubbing hard probably won't be necessary, but if there are particularly stubborn spots go at them with a stiff-bristled brush.

Vinegar-Based Daily Shower Spray

The idea behind a daily shower spray is to keep your tub and shower walls mold, mildew, and soap scum-free between deep cleanings. There's no need to wipe or squeegee -- just spray and go! I use the vinegar-based daily shower spray, but have also provided a vinegar-free alternative for those of you who can't stand the smell of that stuff.

Ingredients:

1/2 cup white vinegar

1 1/2 cups water

10 drops essential oil (tea tree and/or lemon mask the smell of vinegar nicely and add anti-mildew power)

Directions:

1.   Add ingredients to a spray bottle and gently swirl to combine.

2.   Spray on all surfaces of your shower/tub daily after use.

Vinegar-Free Daily Shower Spray

This one uses hydrogen peroxide, which degrades quickly when exposed to light. If you don't own dark-colored spray bottles you can use an old hydrogen peroxide bottle -- most nozzles fit right on the bottle!

Ingredients:

1/4 cup hydrogen peroxide

1/4 cup rubbing alcohol

2-3 drops liquid dish detergent (like Dawn)

1 cup water

Directions:

1.   Add ingredients to an opaque spray bottle and gently swirl to combine.

2.   Spray on all surfaces of your shower/tub daily after use.

3.   IMPORTANT: Keep away from flame!

Window and Glass Cleaner

The rubbing alcohol in this mix is excellent at cutting through grime on windows, leaving a streak-free shine.

Ingredients:

1 part rubbing (Isopropyl) alcohol

1 part white vinegar

3 drops non-moisturizing liquid dish detergent (like Dawn)

Empty spray bottle

Newspaper or squeegee

Directions:

1.   In the spray bottle, combine the alcohol, vinegar and dish soap. Swirl to mix without creating foam.

2.   Fold a few sheets of newspaper together like a washcloth. Spray the glass then wipe with the newspaper (or squeegee). It may look streaky at first if you're using newspaper; just keep switching to a dry section and the streaks will disappear.

3.   When cleaning windows, wipe left-to-right on the inside of the windows, and top-to-bottom on the outside of the windows. That way, if you do leave streaks you'll be able to tell which side they're on.

4.   Use a small rubber spatula as a squeegee when cleaning glass objects or narrow windows, wiping it regularly with a dry cloth so you're always using a clean, dry surface to squeegee.

Homemade Laundry Detergent

This recipe costs pennies per load and does a great job of cleaning. You can find all of these ingredients in the laundry aisle of many stores like Target and Wal-Mart.

Ingredients:

1 bar non-moisturizing soap, like Fels Naptha

1 cup washing soda (not baking soda!)

1 cup Borax

10-15 drops essential oils (optional, but nice for fragrance)

Directions:

1.   Grate the soap on a cheese grater using the large holes. This goes faster if you first microwave it for 20 seconds.

2.   Combine all three ingredients in a plastic container with a lid. Be careful when pouring the powders into the bucket -- you don't want to inhale them!

3.   Add essential oils for fragrance if you'd like.

4.   Put the lid on and shake well. Let the powder settle before opening.

5.   To use, add 1-2 tablespoons to the water as your machine fills. That's it! As with all laundry detergents, adding more won't get your clothes cleaner; it will just leave more soap residue on your clothes.

6.   To pre-treat stains: use water to make a paste from a small amount of the detergent powder. Scrub it into the stain and let sit for 30 minutes before laundering.

Furniture Polish

The white vinegar in this mix keeps the olive oil from going rancid.

Ingredients:

1 cup olive oil

1/4 cup white vinegar

3 to 4 drops lemon essential oil

Directions:

1.   Add all ingredients to a spray bottle and shake well.

2.   Spray onto a smooth, lint-free cloth and wipe onto furniture for light polishing.

3.   For heavier cleaning, spray directly onto furniture and buff well using a clean, lint-free cloth.

4.   Store in a cool, dark place and shake well before each use.

Afterword

More From This Author

Thank you for your purchase of this book! I hope you've found it a valuable tool in transforming your home into the clean, organized place you've always wanted it to be.

For even more guidance, please visit my website HousewifeHowTos.Com where you'll find:

> ➤ Free printable weekly cleaning routines
> ➤ Step-by-step advice to removing carpet stains, including pet messes and dried paint.
> ➤ Even more cleaning mixes
> ➤ An entire shopping area listing my recommended equipment and favorite kitchen gadgets

You may also enjoy my other books available on Amazon:

1,001+ Housewife How-To's: Household Hints to Help Homebodies Cook, Clean, Do Laundry, Get Organized, Save Money and MORE! (available in paperback or for the Kindle)

August: A Season of Easy Cooking (available for the Kindle)

30 Recipes Using Cooked Chicken: Real Food Your Family Will Love (available for Kindle)

Got a Kindle?

This book was originally published in a Kindle format which contains hyperlinks to a number of articles on my website, along with a linked list of recommended equipment. If you've purchased the print version via Amazon you can get a copy for your Kindle (or the Kindle app on your phone, tablet, PC or Mac) for just $0.99!